Praise for *Serve to Be Great*

"Matt Tenney has a clarity about the world that is remarkable. His experience and the lessons he learned need to be heard by as many people as possible."

—**Simon Sinek, optimist and author of *Start with Why* and *Leaders Eat Last***

"*Serve to Be Great* draws you in with one of the most powerful stories you'll ever hear, and offers an inspiring path to true greatness as a leader. I encourage anyone who wants to be great to read this book."

—**Jon Gordon, bestselling author of *The Energy Bus*, *The Carpenter*, and *The Seed***

"*Serve to Be Great* is an engaging book about the power of focusing on others. With a gripping narrative about his journey from prisoner to monk to social entrepreneur, Matt Tenney shows how leaders can elevate those around them and make everyone better off in the process."

—**Adam Grant, Wharton professor and bestselling author of *Give and Take***

"I love a true story of redemption, and Matt Tenney shares a powerful one in this book. He transformed a massive mistake into a magnificent obsession with servant leadership. Learn how you can be of greater service and make a bigger difference as a leader whether you have a title or not—read this book."

—**Mark Sanborn, bestselling author of *The Fred Factor* and *You Don't Need a Title to Be a Leader***

"*Serve to Be Great* is one of those rare books that is an enjoyable and inspiring read, and also quite useful for helping you and your team succeed. Applying the ideas in this book will help you and those around you to achieve better long-term results, and make your lives more meaningful and enjoyable along the way."

—**Chip Conley, Founder and former CEO of Joie de Vivre Hotels and *New York Times* bestselling author of *Peak* and *Emotional Equations***

"*Serve to Be Great* provides you with powerful tools for becoming an extraordinary leader who gets results and makes our world a better place. This inspiring book is a must-read for leaders at all levels."

—**Chade-Meng Tan, Jolly Good Fellow of Google and *New York Times* bestselling author of *Search Inside Yourself***

"*Serve to Be Great* is both inspiring and practical. Matt Tenney delivers a powerful narrative that takes you on an incredible journey. The insights from that journey and the examples he shares of truly great leaders will improve your performance, widen your perspective, and raise your leadership game."

—**Skip Prichard, CEO of OCLC and blogger at www.SkipPrichard.com**

"This is an outstanding book full of truly powerful ideas, tools, stories, and advice. I strongly recommend that you read and apply the lessons of *Serve to Be Great*, because in today's business world *only* those who are devoted to serving and inspiring greatness in others will be successful as leaders."

—**John Spence, named one of the Top 100 Business Thought Leaders in America by Trust Across America and author of *Awesomely Simple***

"In a mere four words, Matt Tenney lays down the clearest guidance to anyone seeking to excel as a workplace leader: *Serve to Be Great*. Matt has lived an untraditional life—and brings forth untraditional wisdom that's perfectly timed. Instead of taking as much as we can from employees, it's time to do as much as we can for them."

—**Mark C. Crowley, change agent and author of *Lead from the Heart: Transformational Leadership for the 21st Century***

"In *Serve to Be Great*, Matt Tenney courageously reveals his journey from being self-serving to serving others, and lays out a world of infinite possibilities that awaits the servant leader. In addition to his own story, Matt shares illuminating stories and lessons from many great leaders and their organizations in his inspiring and useful book."

—**Jeff Klein, producer of Conscious Capitalism events and author of the award-winning book *Working For Good***

"*Serve to Be Great* brings a simple yet profound truth brilliantly alive: Great leaders inspire the best in others, and all of us can do this anywhere, anytime. The moving stories and the ideas Tenney shares provide both the inspiration and the tools to help you become an extraordinary leader."

—Michael Carroll, author of *The Mindful Leader* and *Fearless at Work*

"In *Serve to Be Great*, Matt Tenney reveals his greatest failure and how he was able to turn it into something great and beautiful. This book is engaging and inspiring, and it will help you become a great leader regardless of your current position in life."

—Ted Prince, Founder and CEO of the Perth Leadership Institute and author of *The Three Financial Styles of Very Successful Leaders*

"In *Serve to Be Great,* Matt Tenney invites us into his personal journey of transformation—one in which he found value for our workplaces. Tenney leaves little doubt that when we embrace the notion that 'others' matter, we set in place a chain reaction for good. He has provided us a new set of lenses to view old challenges and new opportunities."

—Clifton L. Taulbert, author of *Eight Habits of the Heart*

"*Serve to Be Great* will expand your thinking about leadership. Matt Tenney provides powerful case studies and practical advice about what it takes to be a highly effective leader today."

—Dan Black, author of *The Leadership Mandate* and blogger at danblackonleadership.info

"There's so much to enjoy about this book. With inspiring examples and guidance, Matt reminds us that every moment matters, and that choosing to serve others in these moments is an act that not only makes our work more meaningful but also produces awesome outcomes."

—Chris Marcell Murchison, Vice President for Staff Development and Culture, HopeLab

"Matt Tenney's story of temptation, self-discovery, and rejuvenation will uplift your heart and renew your faith in humanity."

—David Marquet, author of *Turn the Ship Around!*

SERVE
TO BE GREAT

MATT TENNEY

SERVE
TO BE GREAT

LEADERSHIP LESSONS FROM

A PRISON, A MONASTERY,

AND A BOARDROOM

WILEY

For general information about our other products and services, please contact our Customer
Care Department within the United States at (800) 762-2974, outside the United States at
(317) 572-3993 or fax (317) 572-4002.

Wiley publishes in a variety of print and electronic formats and by print-on-demand. Some
material included with standard print versions of this book may not be included in e-books
or in print-on-demand. If this book refers to media such as a CD or DVD that is not
included in the version you purchased, you may download this material at
http://booksupport.wiley.com. For more information about Wiley products, visit
www.wiley.com.

ISBN 978-1-118-86846-1 (cloth); ISBN 978-1-118-86848-5 (ebk);
ISBN 9781-118-86844-7 (ebk)

Printed in the United States of America

10 9 8 7 6 5 4 3 2 1

To my parents—
For your unconditional support

CONTENTS

FOREWORD

For the past several years, I have been implementing a practice that has been very powerful for me. It has also been very powerful for many of the clients with whom I work. The practice is to simply find a word that represents my core focus for the year to come. Three years ago my word was *purpose*. Two years ago it was *surrender*. In 2013, I didn't choose my word. The word chose me.

While driving in my car in late December of 2012, I was listening to the radio and heard the word *serve*. It really stood out to me. When I changed the station, I heard the word *serve* again. I immediately knew it was my word for 2013. Serving others had always been important to me, but 2013 would be the year that my main focus was to serve more frequently and selflessly.

I met Matt Tenney a little more than halfway through 2013. We were both flying from Houston to Jacksonville and ended up sitting next to each other. As we got to know each other, I noticed that Matt used the word *serve* quite frequently.

He spoke of his passion for improving his ability to serve others. He spoke of his vision of a world in which the vast majority of leaders realize that the best way to achieve lasting, high levels of success is to make serving and taking care of others their main focus. And he mentioned that he was working on a book called *Serve to Be Great*.

Needless to say, I did not see this meeting as coincidence. Matt reenergized my focus on serving. And, as we chatted, I realized that one way I could be of service to many people was to help Matt share his message.

In *Serve to Be Great*, Matt draws you in with one of the most powerful stories you will ever read. He helps us see, through his journey, that we can all make the shift from being self-centered to other-centered. He also makes a compelling case that the best way to achieve lasting success as a leader is to focus on serving and taking care of the people on your team.

I certainly agree. Through my work over the years, I have had the honor of working with thousands of leaders of almost all types of organizations. I've worked with coaches in the NFL, the NBA, and at colleges; leaders at many Fortune 500 companies; leaders of school districts; leaders at hospitals; and leaders of nonprofits. Regardless of the type of team or organization, I can say without hesitation that the most significant factor that separates great leaders from the pack is their desire and ability to be of service to others.

I feel honored to have learned from many great leaders of great organizations about the importance of being a leader who serves and takes care of others. But the teacher who had the greatest impact on me was my mother.

Eight years ago, I was taking a walk with my mom near her home in south Florida when I noticed that she was getting tired. My mom and I walked together a lot. She was a fit, walking machine and never got tired, so I knew something was wrong.

"Let's go back to the condo so you can rest," I said.

"No, I want to walk to the store so I can get some food to make you a sandwich for your drive home."

I was headed back to my home in Ponte Vedra Beach and my mom didn't want me to make the drive hungry.

"Okay," I said, knowing she had her mind set. Growing up in a Jewish-Italian family, the one thing you didn't do is argue with Mom about food. To her, food and love were one and the same.

We continued walking and made it to the supermarket. As we walked back, though, I could tell she was getting increasingly tired. By the time we arrived back at her condo, she was exhausted. Nevertheless, the first thing she did was walk into the kitchen to make me a sandwich.

On my drive home I ate the sandwich she made for me, but I didn't think much about it. Now, eight years later, I think about that sandwich a lot because it was the last time I saw my mom alive.

My mom was battling cancer, which was why she was so tired. She didn't tell me how bad it really was, nor did she mention how bleak the odds were for her survival. She was fighting for her life and yet on that day, her biggest priority was to make me a sandwich.

Looking back I realize she wasn't just making me a sandwich. She was showing me what selfless love is all about. She was showing me the essence of leadership.

At her funeral, many of her real estate clients and colleagues came up to me and shared countless stories of all the selfless acts of love my mom showed them as well. Turns out she served her team at work and her clients the same way she served her family.

We often think that great leadership is about big visions, big goals, big actions, and big success. But I learned from my mom that real leadership is about serving others by doing the little things with a big dose of selfless love.

I feel very confident that after you read *Serve to Be Great*, you will know what my mom knew: Big success is a natural side effect of serving others.

I'm also very confident that you will be deeply inspired to become an extraordinary leader who inspires greatness in the people around you, and that you'll have some powerful tools to help you get there.

Jon Gordon

Bestselling author of *The Energy Bus*,
The Carpenter, and
The Seed

INTRODUCTION

D o you aspire to be a highly effective leader who guides your team or your organization to lasting success? Would you like to wake up excited to face each day because you truly enjoy your work and know that you are having a significant positive impact on the world around you?

This is possible for everyone, regardless of title or position. In fact, you can actually train yourself to make this a reality. Although it's not necessarily *easy,* it's a very simple process.

By making a shift in your approach to leadership, you can become a highly effective leader who enjoys your work and makes the world a better place. The shift is simply a matter of gradually becoming more focused on how you can serve others and increasing your capacity to do so. This is great news because it means that being an extraordinary leader does not require you to have an MBA or a PhD. You don't need to be the leading expert in your field or a charismatic "natural-born leader." As Dr. Martin Luther King Jr. said, "Everybody can be great … because anybody can serve."

In this book, you'll find numerous examples, ideas, and tools for applying this simple shift to improve nearly every aspect of your team or organization. This book will focus on helping you create a team culture that:

- Attracts and retains the most talented people in your industry
- Increases team member engagement and productivity

- Increases your team's capacity for innovation
- Delivers world-class customer service
- Achieves a better return on investment from your marketing efforts

A great team culture is arguably the only sustainable competitive advantage that remains in the new economy. After conducting a large study that included over 6,000 managers, Ed Michaels, a director at the consulting giant McKinsey & Co. who helped manage the study, made the valid point that products, ideas, and strategies can all be copied quickly and cheaply in the transparent world in which we live today. His conclusion from the study was that, in the new economy, "all that matters is talent. Talent wins."[1]

But it is not so easy to create and sustain a team culture that talented people want to be part of, and one that stimulates and encourages improved engagement, innovation, customer service, and marketing efforts. We can only create and sustain a culture like that when a fundamental shift occurs in our approach to leadership: the shift we'll explore in this book. Without the sincere aspiration to serve and care for the people around us, any effort to simply copy a great workplace culture cannot be sustained. The heart of such a culture will be missing.

This book will provide a plethora of inspiring examples and ideas for creating a great team culture. You will also find both inspiration and tools for making the shift in your approach to leadership that allows such a culture to be authentic and sustainable. The book is divided into three parts:

Part One: I share the story of how, through rather extreme circumstances, I discovered the power of a life devoted to serving others and how what I learned led me to where I am—helping organizations to develop highly effective leaders who serve and inspire greatness in others.

Part Two: We'll explore the business case for being a leader who is more focused on serving others, and see how such a leader achieves the improved business outcomes previously described.

Part Three: We'll explore ideas and tools for making the shift and for becoming a highly effective leader who is devoted to serving and inspiring greatness in others.

I'm honored to be able to serve you with this book. I hope you enjoy reading it as much as I enjoyed writing it!

Part 1
My Journey from Prisoner to Monk to Social Entrepreneur

1 My Greatest Failure

For much of my life, I believed that the definition of success was financial freedom—not having to work for a living. There is some logic to this belief. If we're financially free, we've made it. If we don't have to work for a living, we're free to do all the things that we enjoy or whatever is most important to us.

As I got older, this belief became stronger and stronger. By the time I finished college and began my career as an officer in the U.S. Marine Corps, achieving financial freedom became a very high priority for me. In fact, I had a goal of achieving financial freedom by the time I turned 30.

With this goal of financial freedom in mind, I became very focused on money. I spent a lot of my spare time studying investment in stocks, bonds, futures, options, and real estate. I studied entrepreneurship and business and management. If I thought it could help me become financially free, I was interested.

Then came the conversation that changed the course of my life.

It was the fall of the year 2000, and I was on deployment with my unit, headed for the Middle East. On this fateful day, I was on liberty in Singapore, hanging out with a friend of mine who I hadn't seen since officer candidates' school. My friend, who we'll call "Bob," was a finance officer. He was in charge of all the money we had on ship.

We were both talking about how although we liked being Marines, we weren't really enjoying our jobs, and we weren't really happy. Suddenly, Bob drastically changed the direction of the conversation. He said, "Well, one interesting thing about my job is the procurement of funds for deployment. You wouldn't believe how easy it was for me to procure the $4.5 million in cash that we have on the ship." Of course, being focused on money, this caught my attention. I immediately asked, "Really? How easy was it?"

Bob explained the process. It sounded too easy.

Curious, I asked him, "Did you ever think about running off with the money?" He said of course the thought had crossed his mind, but he could never actually *do* something like that. I didn't think I could either, but I sure thought it would make a cool story—running off into the sunset with millions of dollars.

My first thought was, "Maybe I could write a bestselling novel about this, and that would be my ticket to financial freedom." Over the next couple of weeks, I asked Bob a lot of questions as different ideas came to mind. I soon realized that I had enough information to write a really good book. In fact, I realized that I had enough information to actually *live* it.

Initially, I didn't seriously entertain the idea of actually trying to do something like that, so I just stuck to writing about it. But over the next four months, things started to change. I had a habit of focusing on what was wrong with my life, instead of appreciating all that was good. I also had a habit of looking for quick solutions to problems. I almost always sought the easy way out of unpleasant situations.

The more I dwelled on the problems in my life, the more appealing a quick and easy solution appeared to be. And because I was already so focused on money, I found lots of ways to rationalize why attempting to defraud the government wasn't such a bad idea. I told myself things like, "Well, you aren't taking anything from a person. This would be a victimless crime."

Eventually, I convinced myself that I should at least find out if would be possible to arrange the delivery. Once I knew if it was possible, I would still be able to decide whether or not I wanted to go through with acquiring the money.

About a month later, in January of 2001, I took the steps needed to arrange the delivery. I forged two documents and faxed them to the Federal Reserve Bank. I followed up with a phone call to ensure receipt, impersonating a finance officer from another unit.

I was told that everything was in order, and that I simply needed to arrange the delivery with Brinks (the armored car company). I faxed the required document to the company, and followed up with a phone call to ensure receipt. The staff at Brinks also told me that everything was in order.

At that point, I had arranged the unauthorized delivery of $2.79 million from the Federal Reserve Bank of Los Angeles to Camp Pendleton Marine Corps Base.

A few days before the delivery was scheduled to take place, I called Brinks to confirm one last time. The person with whom I spoke informed me that he had forgotten about a new policy they had in place. He said that I would need to come to their office and sign a contract for the delivery. So, I had a nametag displaying the name of the officer I was impersonating made and sewn onto one of my uniforms, and went to the office wearing that uniform. I signed the contract—which promised the delivery of $2.79 million the next day—and took a copy with me.

Although this might sound like the script of some thrilling movie, the actual experience was terribly unpleasant. I was almost overcome by anxiety. With each subsequent act of dishonesty came an increasing amount of sickness in my stomach.

Once I had the contract from Brinks in my hand, reality finally hit me in the face. I said to myself, "What the heck are you doing, man?! You aren't a criminal! You don't even have a plan for picking up this money! Are you crazy?!" At that point, I abandoned the whole idea and shredded the contract with Brinks on my way home.

I knew that it wouldn't be long before someone figured out that this was all a hoax. Fear set in. Since I had been to Brazil a couple times and knew the language, I decided to go there and find out from a nice, safe distance whether or not I was in any trouble. I bought a one-way ticket, packed as though I was going on vacation, and went to the bank and withdrew all the cash I had, which was less than $5,000. I went to Walmart to pick up a suitcase and some warm-weather clothes.

After leaving the store, as I approached my Jeep, some girls pointed to a man standing by a parked car and said, "That guy is following you." When I started to walk toward the man, he got in his car and sped away. Because I didn't think there was any way authorities could have been aware of what I had done—and because of the way the man drove off—I didn't think that he was with the authorities. But authorities *were* aware of what I had done. While I was signing the contract at Brinks, FBI agents had placed a tracking device on my Jeep, and it was actually an FBI agent who was following me at Walmart. As I was on my way to the airport the next morning, the FBI began following me again. When I was within a couple of miles of John Wayne Airport in Orange County, I was pulled over by unmarked cars, yanked out of my Jeep at gunpoint by an FBI takedown team, and arrested.

Although this sounds absolutely frightening, I actually felt better that day than I had felt in over a month. I told the FBI everything. It felt so good to finally tell the truth. After spending most of the day with the FBI, I was taken to the Federal Detention Center in San Diego. I spent about a week there before the Marine Corps took jurisdiction of my case and I was transferred to the base brig (a military prison) at Camp Pendleton.

Understandably, the Marine Corps was not happy with me. I had dishonored what is perhaps the most honorable organization on the planet. I was placed in a six-foot by nine-foot cell. During the nearly six months while I awaited my court-martial, I spent an average of 22 hours per day alone in that cell—essentially in solitary confinement.

This was the worst experience of my life. I probably went through every negative emotion humanly possible during this experience. But it was mostly anger—at myself. I remember thinking, "You idiot, what the heck were you thinking? You've thrown your whole life away." I also quickly realized that my crime was *not* a victimless one, as I had assumed. I caused suffering for the Marines who had looked to me as their leader. I also caused suffering for my friends, for my peers, and for my leaders.

But the ones who suffered the most were probably my family. I shocked and embarrassed them. Even worse, I caused them a tremendous amount of worry and fear. I can't imagine what it must have been like for my parents to think of their son being in prison, or for my sister to think of her brother there. I hadn't considered any of these things while arranging the delivery, so I was absolutely furious at myself for being so selfish.

The worst day of all was the day my military lawyer came to visit me for the first time. He sat down outside my cell door. We had to talk to each other through a slot used to pass food into the cell, which measured about 3 inches high and 12 inches wide. I asked him, "How long do you think I could be here?" I'm not really sure I wanted to know the answer. He replied, "Matthew, the charges total up to 85 years. You could possibly spend 70 or 80 years in the brig."

I went into a sort of shock. I spent the rest of the day in a daze. I was so mad and so depressed that for the first time in my life I actually had thoughts of suicide flashing through my mind. Although I never tried to hurt myself, for weeks I went to sleep at night with tears in my eyes, silently praying, "Please don't let me wake up in the morning. Please, just don't let me wake up in the morning."

Finding Opportunity in Disaster

After a few months, I found out that I wasn't going to be there 70 or 80 years. In order to avoid the time and expense of a trial, the government asked me to sign a pretrial agreement in which I agreed to admit guilt and the government agreed to cap my confinement at eight years. I gladly signed the agreement. Also, most confinement facilities offer a slight reduction in sentence to reward good behavior. Thus, as long as I followed the rules, I would be confined to military prison for about six years.

Although that still seemed like a really long time, I could at least wrap my head around it. As I began to come to terms with my sentence, I started to consciously look for what opportunities might be found in this situation. After all, I would have six years of days—all day every day—to myself. I would have a lot of time to think.

Initially, despite the extreme consequences that resulted from focusing on money, I still defined success as having financial freedom. So, my first thought was to develop a legitimate plan for achieving financial freedom after leaving the brig. I studied more on investing and business, I read books by Robert Kiyosaki and other financial freedom gurus. After a couple months, I felt that I had a pretty realistic plan for attaining my goals within a short time of being released from confinement. But I also knew that it would be six years before I could put the plan into action, so I set it aside.

In the weeks and months that followed my mind eventually began to wander to the deeper questions of life. One of those questions was the focus of many, many hours of contemplation, probably because it was something I could actually test out right there where I was. I wondered if it was possible to be just as happy in the brig, with no real possessions or comforts, as I could be if I were not physically confined. Although I thought it was highly unlikely, the idea was intriguing. If I could learn to be happy where I was, then even an average life outside of the brig would probably seem like heaven on Earth.

As I contemplated this, I remembered that I had once heard about monks who give up all their possessions and choose to live a life like the one I was forced to live. They do so because they have faith in their teachers, who make it clear that living such a life actually makes it easier to realize true happiness. I didn't know why this was so, but just recognizing that whole groups of people did such a thing gave me hope. I decided that it must be possible to be just as happy in the brig as I could be anyplace else.

Very fortunately for me, about one year into my sentence, I started learning about a simple practice called *mindfulness*, through books that my mother sent to me. I learned that the practice was originally created to end suffering and allow people to realize true happiness—the kind that comes from within and does not depend on anything outside of oneself. It seemed that mindfulness just might be exactly what I was looking for.

The foundation of this practice is essentially awareness training. We're training ourselves to not be distracted by our thinking. We've all had the experience of trying to pay attention in a class or a meeting, and then a thought crosses our mind and distracts us. That leads to another thought, which leads to another. Before we know it, minutes go by and we realize we have no idea what anyone said during the last 10 minutes! Chances are, this has happened to you—and it's okay. It happens to all of us.

Awareness training is simply making the effort, whenever we remember, to notice *what's happening now,* without judgment, and without getting pulled completely into our thinking. For example, just notice what it's like to sit where you are right now. What does your chair feel like? What do you hear right now? What do you see? What does it feel like to breathe in and out?

We're not trying to eliminate thinking or block thoughts out; we're just training to not be distracted by our thinking. Imagine how much more effective you would be in so many areas of life if you were no longer distracted by your thinking. There is likely a whole list of ways that you would benefit from this kind of focus, both personally and professionally.

But what initially attracted me to the practice was a very simple, logical idea that I read in a book from one of the most well-known teachers of mindfulness in the world, an individual named Thich Nhat Hanh. The idea was this: If we're not comparing the present moment to thoughts of the past or thoughts of the future, the present moment is actually perfect just as it is.

Imagine that you are in a brig cell sitting on your bed. You are not in any pain, you are not hungry, and the temperature is comfortable. If you're not comparing that moment to memories of the past, or hopes for the future, what's wrong with that moment?

Nothing. The problems don't start until the mind kicks in and starts telling us how much better things will be in the future, when we are free from confinement. We all face variations of this issue on a daily basis. We're always thinking about what's *next*, and how much happier we'll be once we get *there*.

It didn't take me long to see how awareness training sets us free from the pull of our comparative thinking. That insight was accompanied by a very liberating thought: Awareness training could help me to be happy under *any* circumstances, even while I was in the brig.

If I could be free from comparative thinking while brushing my teeth, for instance, then brushing my teeth in the cell would be no different than brushing my teeth at home. I would be free in that moment. If I could be free while brushing my teeth, I could also be free while walking, cleaning my cell, working, or during any other activity.

Within a short time, I was practicing awareness training during just about every moment of the day. After about six months of diligent practice, I noticed that I was thriving in one of the most stressful environments in the world. In fact, I was happier right there in the brig than I had ever been in my entire life. After spending my whole life looking outside myself for happiness, I learned firsthand that we already have within us everything that we need to be happy. And we can actually train ourselves to realize that.

2 From Selfish to Servant

Most of the books I read in the brig were written by monks. They explained how monastic training can speed up personal development. Since following their teachings had allowed me to find true happiness in the brig, I had a tremendous amount of faith in their guidance. So I decided to go all the way. I spent the last three years of my sentence living and training just like a monk.

After about a year into my time in confinement, I was transferred to another brig and allowed to live in the general population. This made life in the brig a bit more "normal." We went to work each day as most people do. In our free time, we had access to books, magazines, music, television, movies, and games.

But I decided to give up all the vain amusements we could use to distract ourselves and followed the strict rules monks do. The rules include living as simply as possible, not seeking out entertainment, and being as virtuous and selfless as possible. I devoted myself entirely to the training. I diligently practiced awareness training during nearly every moment of the day, including long periods each day of practicing while sitting still in silence.

In essence, I turned the brig into a monastery—my own training center for personal development. I've referred to this experience as my "monastery experience" ever since. In fact, I call it my "monastery on steroids," because in a regular monastery, it's very quiet and people treat you nicely. I had the benefit of living simply. However, it was also obnoxiously loud almost all the time, and many of the staff members often treated us poorly, as though we had no value in the world and never would. So, I had all types of opportunities to experience anger and frustration.

I realized pretty quickly that the more often I faced my anger with full awareness, the freer I was from it. I actually started to become grateful for difficult situations and people because I knew that they were helping me learn to master myself. Gradually, I noticed that negative emotions like anger, fear, and anxiety were losing their strength and arising less and less. This opportunity to face such emotions so frequently was an incredible blessing in disguise.

Perhaps the most important development of monastic training for me was that my reason for practicing—my motivation—shifted: Instead of focusing on my own happiness—since I was already very happy—I began focusing more on helping the people around me to be happy. I took on the vow that is common in one form or another in most monastic traditions: to help all people to be free from suffering.

This vow gradually became a new purpose for my life, a purpose that was much bigger than myself: to help all people to be free from suffering, starting with the people around me in the brig. I reminded myself of that purpose every day, numerous times each day.

This constant reminder completely changed my experience of the brig. While many people there were miserable, hoping that the time would go as quickly as possible so they could get out and get on to whatever was next, I woke up every morning excited to face the day simply because I had a purpose that was bigger than myself. I actually woke up an hour early to devote extra time to my training.

My heroes changed, too. They became people like Jesus, Gandhi, the Dalai Lama, Mother Theresa, Thich Nhat Hanh, and Martin Luther King Jr. I realized that these people are the epitome of true greatness, and I wanted to be just like them.

I was so enamored by the ideal of the monastic life that after leaving in the summer of 2006—after serving five and one-half years in the brig—I actually moved into a monastery, and lived there for six weeks. I came very, very close to ordaining as a monk for the rest of my life. But a sudden insight prevented me from actually ordaining. I realized that although for many people becoming a monk would be an incredible sacrifice, for me it was taking the easy way out. I had already lived like a monk for years, with no possessions, no fun, and no girlfriend, and I was very happy. Living like that would not be a challenge for me. I knew that if I wanted to grow more as a human being and be better able to serve others, I would need to continue living and training as a monk—but in the "real world." I needed to face the same challenges everyone else does.

But all I wanted to do was help people, so I started looking for ways that I could serve. I wasn't really clear on how to best do that, so I decided to go learn a second language and serve in whatever way I could until the best path revealed itself.

I didn't have much money saved, so I decided to go to a lovely city on the Pacific coast of Mexico called Mazatlàn, where the cost of living was pretty low. I stayed at a hotel on the beach while looking for an apartment. On my third day there, I had a nice conversation with one of the employees, named Javier, and mentioned that I would like to do volunteer work with orphans or other disadvantaged youth. Javier's aunt happened to be the director for a special school for disadvantaged youth. Nearly all of the boys at the school lived in a nearby orphanage.

Javier arranged for me to meet with his aunt, Maria. Despite my inability to communicate in Spanish at that point, the meeting went well. Maria welcomed me to help out at the school as an English teacher and assistant to the teacher who worked with the first and second graders. Although I couldn't understand most of her words, I definitely got the message. I didn't need to be a fluent Spanish speaker, because what these kids needed more than anything was love. I felt honored that Maria sensed a capacity for care and love in me that gave her confidence in my ability to make a difference in the lives of the children she loved as though they were her own.

I ended up developing a great relationship with Maria and her family, and she became very confident in my abilities to help children develop both academically and psychosocially. So, when I told her that I would like to find volunteer work over the summer, she arranged for me to meet with the director of a shelter for children who had been neglected or abused, and either taken from their homes by the state or abandoned by their parents. The meeting went well, and I was asked to create a summer school program for the children at the shelter.

Just as with the school, what those children needed most was unconditional love. They had lived incredibly difficult lives and were often victims of rather horrific abuse. And, although the shelter was a safe place for them, it was not a very comfortable place to be. It looked more like a prison than a home. The small outdoor common area consisted of almost entirely concrete, surrounded by tall walls and fences topped with barbed wire, with only three small trees in concrete planters.

I saw my task of creating and teaching a summer school program as a cover, of sorts, that allowed me to do the real work of simply loving the children at the shelter, helping them deal with the powerful emotions that often surfaced, and encouraging them to see the value in treating each other with kindness. Although this work was very challenging at times, it was also one of the most rewarding things I have done.

After nine months in Mazatlàn, I felt that I had gained some clarity on how I could best apply my life experiences to serve others. As much as I loved working with children, I decided that I should apply my own experience to help people in confinement transform prison into an opportunity to realize freedom from suffering. I had come to realize that happy people don't do things to intentionally hurt others. Only people who are suffering do that. Thus, if we focus more on relieving prisoners' suffering instead of only punishing them, we could decrease the likelihood that these people would commit another crime when they are released and lower the high recidivism rate.

My initial plan was to continue working with children during the day while I began learning about working with people in prison in the evenings. I moved home and began applying for teaching positions. In one day of interviewing with principals,

I had two offers to teach in middle schools. Although I shared the story of my past, the school's principals told me that it was obvious from my volunteer work in Mexico that my failure had taught me tremendously and that I would be great for the youth in their schools.

Unfortunately, I learned after I had interviewed that the school district had recently adopted a policy against hiring anyone with any type of criminal background, even if the offense was not against a person. Although I was disappointed, I understood their policy.

I started looking for people who were already doing the work in prisons that I had in mind and found that there was a man in Gainesville, Florida, who had developed a very extensive program he used to rehabilitate people confined to prison. After meeting with him, he asked me to work voluntarily as the executive director of the small nonprofit that served as the base for the program. I was happy to serve and honored that I was given a position of such responsibility so soon after leaving confinement.

I took a simple customer service job at a printing company to support myself, and started the process of getting cleared to work in the prisons. Then I had another disappointing discovery: There is a state law that prohibits people who have been confined from volunteering inside a Florida prison until three years after the person was released. Again, although I was disappointed, I understood. I simply kept moving forward, trying to think of other ways I could serve.

I founded my own 501(c)(3) nonprofit with the mission of reducing crime rates and rates of recidivism, and built a board of directors to help run the organization. Since I couldn't work inside the prisons, our organization distributed a book I wrote on finding happiness while confined. The book was sent to inmates for free. Eventually, we decided that we should shift our focus to offering programs that could help prevent people from offending in the first place.

We offered a program for disadvantaged youth in which participants learned awareness training and other personal development tools through the martial arts. It was called the Ultimate Warrior Program. The program's primary goal was to get young people's attention by offering to teach them the mixed martial arts techniques they see in events like the Ultimate Fighting Championship, but impress upon them the truth that the "ultimate warrior" is not the one who has mastered the fists; it's the one who has mastered the mind. The ultimate warrior, we taught them, trains to defeat the true enemies of greed, anger, and hate.

Around the same time, I was offered a sales position at an energy company that has been voted numerous times to be one of the best companies to work for in Florida, which just happened to be located in Gainesville. Although I never would have thought that I would enjoy a sales position, I really liked it. I realized that the essence of sales is to help meet the legitimate needs of another person or a business. With that approach, a sales position can actually be a great opportunity to serve. As a result of this focus on service, I did pretty well and was promoted to be a sales team leader after just six months on the job.

During this busy time, I continued to run the nonprofit while juggling a full-time job. I was also teaching or co-teaching all of the classes we offered, which included classes for the school system and for an after-school program run by the Gainesville Police Department, called the Reichert House, which helps underprivileged youth develop skills for success in life.[1]

After running the Ultimate Warrior program for a couple years, I was invited to be the instructor for a similar program that teaches mindfulness and breathing techniques through the martial arts. This particular program serves youth fighting serious illnesses and their families. The focus for this initiative—created by an international nonprofit organization (NPO) called Kids Kicking Cancer[2]—is not behavior modification. Rather, it's to help these young people lower their own pain levels and realize greater peace of mind.

Within a short time, I realized that I was going to be doing a lot more than just teaching the classes. The Gainesville program is a joint effort between Kids Kicking Cancer and a local nonprofit called UF Health Shands Arts in Medicine.[3] A lot of coordination needed to take place between the two organizations, as well as with the hospital staff.

In January of 2011, I decided to leave my position as sales team leader and focus all my energy on my nonprofit work. I ended up becoming the co-founder and program director for the Gainesville chapter of Kids Kicking Cancer[4] and, eventually, we merged the nonprofit I founded with the Kids Kicking Cancer program. In addition to getting to work regularly with some incredible young heroes, who often inspire me and teach me more than I teach them, I also managed volunteers and employees and built an advisory board to help ensure that the program would be sustainable for years to come.

The Practice That Changed My Life

Throughout this time, I realized the more focused I became on how I could serve others, the happier I became and the more successful I was. Despite having a felony on my record, job and business opportunities have seemed to come very easily. It seems that most people I meet offer to help me once it becomes clear to them that my focus in life is helping others. I've also noticed that the purer my intentions are—the less focused I am on what's in it for me, and the more focused I am on how I can be most helpful—the more magical my life has become.

When reflecting on this during the fall of 2012, I became clear on a simple way to articulate the core practice that has made the biggest difference in my life: Whether consciously or unconsciously, I've been filtering every decision that I make through the question, "How will this help me to serve others?" If I can't find a direct link between how something I'm about to do will help someone else, I simply don't do it. Of course, I'm not perfect at this practice, but this is the direction that guides me.

I'm not saying that we must be actively serving other people during all of our waking hours. Most of us would burn out pretty quickly if we tried to do that. I'm suggesting that we simply spend less time seeking out ways to entertain ourselves and accumulate money and possessions, and spend more time seeking out ways we can serve the people around us. Ultimately, we should make serving others the motivation for *everything* that we do. This shift is incredibly powerful.

What If Businesses Operated in This Way?

When I reflected on the positive effects in both my personal and professional life that resulted from making serving others the motivation for everything I do, another question followed: "I wonder what would happen if *businesses* operated in this way?"

It occurred to me that if business leaders (or leaders of any organization, for that matter) were 100 percent focused on how they could serve not only customers but also the employees they lead, they would achieve tremendous success. Adopting this mentality would allow companies to build trust and loyalty with their customers. It would also result in increased empathy for their customers, which would help companies provide better customer service. It could even uncover additional customer needs, thereby prompting the creation and offering of additional products or services.

If leaders focused on serving employees, did whatever they could to help them be happier at work and at home, and helped them to continually develop both professionally and personally, those employees would be much more engaged at work. This would result in better performance, increased productivity, better products, and better customer service.

My curiosity about this approach led me to start doing research to see whether there were any businesses that currently operated in this way. As it turns out, there is an entire philosophy of leadership based on this idea of serving others, which is very appropriately called *servant leadership*. Being a servant leader doesn't mean that we assume some menial, meek persona. Rather, motivated by the aspiration to serve, servant leaders achieve true power by empowering others to achieve great things.

The Power of Servant Leadership

Many highly successful companies are already practicing servant leadership. Every year, *Fortune* magazine publishes a list of the top 100 companies to work for. Obviously, all of those that make the list emphasize the importance of caring for employees and helping them grow. Typically, though, about a third of them explicitly state that they intentionally practice servant leadership throughout their organization.

One of the most well-known examples of a company that intentionally practices servant leadership is Southwest Airlines.[5] Southwest was one of the first companies to state publicly that employees, not shareholders, are their top priority. The leaders at Southwest are known for truly loving the people in their organization and working hard to serve them.

Former CEO Herb Kelleher was known for doing things like coming in on Thanksgiving day to work side by side with baggage handlers and help them load suitcases onto the planes. Herb believed that the best way to run a company was with love. Southwest calls themselves the "airline that love built"; you can even see the heart in their logo.

Has Southwest succeeded with this formula of running a company with love? I would say so. In fact, relative to their industry, Southwest is one of the most successful companies in history.

They typically have costs that are half of the industry average. Declaring bankruptcy is a common practice in the airline industry, and most companies are happy to have one profitable year every now and then. But Southwest has been profitable every single year for over 40 consecutive years. And even though they started relatively recently with just a couple of airplanes, Southwest's market value during much of Herb Kelleher's time there was typically about three times the value of all of the other major U.S. airlines *combined*.

Another well-known company that practices servant leadership and leads with love is Herschend Family Entertainment

(HFE).[6] Joel Manby, the CEO at HFE and the author of *Love Works: Seven Timeless Principles for Effective Leaders,*[7] became pretty famous a few years ago after he appeared on the hit TV series *Undercover Boss*. He worked alongside several frontline employees and learned of the struggles they were facing. The show ended with Joel offering some incredible assistance to these employees.

There was a young man who had actually stated on camera that he planned to be CEO of HFE one day. Joel helped him get a scholarship from HFE that would allow him to be paid his full salary to go to school full time. He helped a woman who was homeless when she first started working at the company get a raise and have her apartment furnished. He helped a man who had five kids and whose home was destroyed in a flood get a $10,000 grant to get back on his feet.

That episode had around 80 million viewers, and many of them were deeply moved by seeing the CEO of a large company act with such compassion. Joel was flooded with letters and requests for interviews, and was soon offered a book deal. But the way he treated employees in that episode was pretty much just business as usual at HFE.

Joel believes that "leading with love" is the best form of leadership for any organization. HFE actually uses love to define their leadership culture; they even have a formal leadership development program called Leading with Love. Joel doesn't mean *love* the feeling, but *love* the action, the verb. We don't have to like someone to treat that person with kindness and respect, and to extend ourselves to help her be happy and grow as a human being.

The results of leading with love have been incredible for HFE. During the seven years prior to Joel's book being published—which included the worst recession in our country since the Great Depression—HFE grew its operating profit by over 50 percent and earned an average annual return for its investors of 14 percent.

The Essence of Leadership

Clearly, leading with a focus on serving others goes a long way in helping an organization achieve sustainable success. This approach has been called the most powerful leadership principle in the world. In fact, there is an excellent book on servant leadership, written by leadership expert James Hunter, called *The World's Most Powerful Leadership Principle*.[8] In his book, Hunter provides a very logical explanation for why servant leadership is so effective: *influence*.

Being a leader has nothing to do with having a title. If a person has a title but no one is following him, then that person is not a leader. Leaders are those who influence people's behaviors. There is no better way to build our influence with others than to serve them. People are much more likely to follow us when they know that we truly care about and want to help them.

Another story about Southwest's Herb Kelleher illustrates the power of influence. About halfway through 2000, it appeared as though the company was not going to have a profitable year for the first time in their 30-year history. They did the math and figured out that the only way to be profitable was if each person in the company could save, on average, about $5 per day for the rest of the year.

Herb wrote a letter that read something like this and sent it to every employee in the company:

Dear Friends,

We've had a great run of 30 consecutive years of profitability, but it looks like we're not going to make it this time. The only way we will is if each one of you could find a way to save five dollars a day for the rest of the year. Would you please try to do that?

What's notable is how he signed the letter:

Love, Herb

It's notable because he meant it—and everyone knew it. They remembered all the ways he demonstrated his love over the years, like coming in on Thanksgiving to help the baggage handlers. You can probably guess what happened: People saved $5 a day, and Southwest had yet another profitable year. That's the kind of influence we create when people know we truly care about them.

Serving by Helping Organizations Develop Extraordinary Leaders

As I accumulated evidence that serving and caring for the people on their teams allowed organizations to achieve better business outcomes, I wondered whether there was an opportunity for me to serve on an even larger scale. I realized that helping organizations to achieve better business outcomes by developing leaders who are better able to serve and care for team members could have a significant impact on our society.

As a growing number of companies flourished under this model, I wondered—and reasoned—that this approach could become ubiquitous. It could be something that we would all

eventually consider to be the best way to run an organization. I'm
sure you could imagine the almost endless positive effects this
would have on our society as a whole.

This idea really inspired me: Running a successful organization and doing things that make our world a better place are not
mutually exclusive. In fact, the two can actually create a syner-
gistic effect in which one dramatically improves the other! With
this as my motivation, I launched my own speaking and training
company. I wanted to help organizations make the connection
between serving others and achieving better business outcomes,
inspire leaders to become more focused on serving others, and
provide practical ideas and tools, based on my expertise, for
actually making that happen.

Very fortunately for me, I met Dr. Ted Prince—the founder
and CEO of the prestigious Perth Leadership Institute[9]—within
a short time of starting my business. Perth's clients include
numerous Fortune 500 companies, and the institute has been
ranked in the top 25 leadership development firms in the
world by *Leadership Excellence* magazine. Dr. Prince invited
me to undergo the certification process for becoming a trainer
for the Perth Leadership Institute, which I did. The research
that the institute conducted pointed to a very interesting
link between mindfulness training and increasing profitable
behaviors—something that really caught my attention. I also
I knew that this would give me another tool to help organizations
achieve better business outcomes, and add an excellent credential
that would allow me to serve more organizations.

As I started to get out and serve organizations through my
speaking and training work, I noticed a wonderful side effect.
I started learning about or meeting the leaders of highly successful

organizations that are focused on serving first. You'll meet many of these leaders in Part Two of this book. Their examples will make it crystal clear that concentrating on serving others and increasing your capacity to do so can improve nearly every area of your team or organization—especially in the following areas on which I will focus:

- Attracting and retaining the most talented people in your industry
- Increasing engagement and productivity
- Increasing your team's capacity for innovation
- Delivering world-class customer service
- Achieving a better return on investment from your marketing efforts

I also hope that these leaders will inspire you to achieve extraordinary results and offer you some great ideas that you can implement in your team or organization to achieve similar outcomes.

Part 2
Serve to Be Great: The Business Case

3 Winning the War for Talent

The fall of 2012 was an incredibly exciting time for me. In October, I met the well-known author and speaker Simon Sinek at the annual Inc. 500 conference. Simon had been a hero of mine for years, so I would have been happy just to have a brief conversation with him. But, to my surprise and delight, we actually hit it off immediately and became friends. I met with him for lunch for nearly two hours, and he invited me to come to New York so that he could introduce me to some people that shared our vision of improving our world by helping businesses see the connection between serving people and the greater good and achieving high levels of success.

At the same conference, I also met Scott Harrison, the founder of charity: water,[1] which is an amazing, highly innovative NPO that, as of this writing, has helped 3.3 million people in 20 developing countries gain access to clean drinking water. As Scott and I talked, I learned that he was very good friends with Simon. When I mentioned that Simon had invited me to New York, Scott suggested that I should come in December for charity: water's annual fundraising gala, called charity: ball, because

Simon would be there and it would be a great opportunity for the three of us to get together.

The night of the gala, I arrived in New York City for the first time in my life. After settling in to my Manhattan hotel room, which was about the size of a walk-in closet, I headed out to charity: ball. That night, Simon introduced to me one of the people he wanted me to meet: Charlie Kim, the founder and CEO of an e-commerce company called Next Jump.[2] I was captivated by Charlie and wanted to learn more about his company. I would have the chance the following day. Simon informed me that I would be going with him to a meeting at Next Jump on Tuesday afternoon.

Tuesday was incredible. The first highlight was a one-on-one lunch with Simon. After lunch, he took me to meet his publisher. That meeting was followed by our trip to Simon's office at Next Jump.

When we arrived at Next Jump around 5:00 p.m., we were escorted to the conference room where Simon was going to be interviewed by culture expert Jill Felska. Even though I had been a fan of Simon's for years and had spent much of the previous 24 hours with him, I learned a great deal from listening to this interview. After the interview, Charlie offered to give Jill and me a tour of Next Jump, and we gladly accepted.

It became obvious almost immediately that there was something very different about this company. Most founders or CEOs would begin such a tour or other type of presentation about their company by talking about what the company does. But that's not how Charlie began. In fact, after the 45-minute tour had ended, I still had no idea what Next Jump does. I actually had to research it when I got home the next day.[3]

Charlie focused his discussion on how the leaders at Next Jump work in so many ways to serve and care for their employees, and help them grow personally and professionally. The first stop we made on our tour was an entire wall devoted to recognizing the company's uniqueness. It featured the employees who had earned awards for various types of excellent performance, and focused on the process behind the performance instead of the actual outcome. Charlie began by pointing out a picture of young woman and her groom, in wedding attire, surrounded by a group of about 75 people.

The woman in the photo, Nadia, was a Next Jump employee. She was really concerned about taking people away from work, so she had only invited a couple of Next Jump employees (called NxJumpers) to her wedding, which would take place on a Thursday at City Hall. When Charlie found out about this, he told everyone that the New York City office would close down so that they could surprise Nadia by going to the wedding. When an employee at city hall discovered that Nadia was essentially a secretary at Next Jump, he asked Charlie why he would close down his entire headquarters to come the wedding of a secretary. Charlie said, "Where I come from, when somebody in your family gets married, you go to the wedding."

Many leaders claim to treat the people on their teams like family. The leaders at Next Jump actually do.

Next Jump's leaders are also committed to creating an extraordinary workplace culture, which they summarize succinctly with the simple motto: Better Me + Better You = Better Us. "Better Me" refers to all the things that the leaders at Next Jump do to care for their employees to help them grow both personally and professionally. "Better You" refers to all the initiatives aimed at encouraging NxJumpers to help each other, as well as the community outside of Next Jump. This all results in a "Better Us": a company that achieves superior business outcomes while also developing people of high character who are making the world a better place. The leaders at Next Jump are building a culture of people who, motivated by the aspiration to help others, are driven to become the best human beings they can be.

Although similar to the famous culture at Google and other organizations that take excellent care of people, I believe that the culture at Next Jump leads the pack. Like the leaders at other organizations with great cultures, Charlie and the other leaders at Next Jump spend a lot of time looking for ways to make the lives of NxJumpers better.

Like Google and others, Next Jump has free, healthy food for employees and an on-site gym, complete with personal trainers and a litany of different classes. The company offers a plethora of in-house paid training that helps employees grow personally and professionally. This effort to develop employees includes an initiative called Next Jump University, which consists of a wide array of classes taught by outside experts, as well as talks from high-profile thought leaders that one would typically only hear at a large conference. Next Jump also runs an innovative mentoring program that actually *works* (despite the research indicating that the majority of mentoring programs don't work well).

The leaders at Next Jump don't stop there. They also make it a habit to regularly ask employees what the company can do to help them be happier both at work and at home. Whenever the leadership hears two or more NxJumpers express the same idea, they look into whether the idea has true merit and whether it would be feasible to execute.

In 2010, a few employees mentioned that living in New York City meant they often spent about half of every other weekend in a laundromat. Charlie realized that if his employees enjoy their weekends more, they'll be happier and more productive at work. So he asked how much it would cost for the company to do the employees' laundry. He was informed that NxJumpers weren't asking the company to pay for it. They just wanted the company to facilitate the process so that they could enjoy their weekends more.

Nevertheless, Charlie asked the team to go ahead and look into how much it would cost to do the employees' laundry because he saw an opportunity to further demonstrate how much the leaders at Next Jump care for the people in their organization. They learned that dry cleaning would be prohibitively expensive. They also learned that although standard washing was also costly, it was feasible. Thus, in 2010, Next Jump started its free, weekly laundry program, available to all employees. Employees can drop off their laundry bag in the office on Fridays every week. Their laundry is washed, dried, and folded over the weekend and can be picked up the following Monday. The employees carry their laundry back and forth in bright orange bags that have the Next Jump logo on them. Below the logo are the words, "My company gets my laundry, I get my weekends back."

What truly distinguishes Next Jump is the strong emphasis they place on their effort to build an entire culture of people devoted to helping others, which is emphasized by the "better you/better us" component. Perhaps the most impressive example of the leaders' commitment is the inception of something they call the Avenger Award: a $30,000 package that includes a third week of paid vacation. This award doesn't go to the top programmer, or the top salesperson. Rather, it goes to the person who is voted by his or her peers to be the most helpful, selfless person in the company. The award is given to the best servant leader.

There is a good deal of evidence that the leaders at Next Jump are succeeding in creating a culture of people devoted to helping others. I attended the July 2013 ceremony when a NxJumper named Gowri was announced as the winner of the Avenger Award, so I got to see the NxJumpers' reactions firsthand. You would think there might be hard feelings or jealousy when someone wins $30,000. But when Gowri was announced, he received a standing ovation from the tearful audience of 300 people, which included his parents, who the company had flown in from India to see him receive this honor.[4]

One result of creating the kind of environment that Next Jump has is that people become extremely effective at working as a team. When people think more in terms of "us," teams become much stronger and much more successful. An organization that works better as a team, and has very cohesive subteams as a result, has a significant advantage over one composed of members who are more focused on their individual needs. A group of smart people working together creates a level of intelligence far greater than what each individual has to offer alone.

Attracting Top Talent

Creating a culture like Next Jump's is arguably the only sustainable competitive advantage that exists in today's new economy. It allows companies to develop advantages that are very difficult to copy, like improving our capacity for innovation and delivering world-class customer service. But in order to hone and offer those advantages, we have to be able to attract the right *people* to the organization. Without good team members, companies will be destined to fail.

Next Jump is extremely effective at attracting the right people. In 2012, they accepted only 35 new hires out of almost 18,000 applicants. That's an acceptance rate of 0.2 percent. To give you a bit of comparison, the acceptance rate at Harvard in 2012 was 5.9 percent. In 2012, it was roughly 30 times easier to get accepted into Harvard than it was to get a job at Next Jump.

This incredible ability to attract potential employees means that Next Jump was able to narrow down the number of potential candidates from a pool of almost 18,000 applicants to a group of several hundred extremely smart, extremely talented people. To work at Next Jump in a skilled position, it's essentially a prerequisite that you finish in the top 1 percent of your university class. But that's not enough. From that pool of several hundred of the most talented people in the industry, Next Jump was able to choose the 35 people who are the best fit for their culture—driven, humble individuals who are passionate about helping others.

Fully Engaged People

Once you have the right people on your team, you also need to ensure that those people are fully engaged while they're at work. Otherwise, that talent is wasted—along with a lot of money.

According to a 2005 survey conducted by America Online and Salary.com, the average worker admits to wasting a little over two hours during an eight-hour workday, not including lunch and scheduled break time. According to Salary.com, this means that employers spend $759 billion per year on salaries for which real work was expected, but not actually performed.[5]

To get a number that you can actually use in your organization to calculate the profit or loss from employees, you can apply the findings of a study conducted by the Human Capital Institute. The study showed that disengaged employees return in value only 60 to 80 percent of their salaries. Conversely, fully engaged employees return in value approximately 120 percent of their salaries.

Building a culture like the one at Next Jump is a very effective way to ensure that people are fully engaged and highly productive while they're at work. Next Jump employees are so engaged that they actually requested to have two bedrooms put into the New York City office so they could sleep over on nights when they stay late working on a project. When Charlie first heard this, his immediate response was, "No way! People are going to think I'm running a sweat shop!"

But the NxJumpers were really adamant about it, and they made a sound argument: They frequently stay late working on projects that they're really excited about, and they didn't want to have to take the subway back and forth and lose hours of sleep on those nights. After taking some time to think about it, Charlie decided that this would be a sound investment. There are now two bedrooms in the New York City office.

Can you imagine having employees so engaged that they *ask* to be able to spend the night at the office? I'm not sure it is possible to quantify the return in value employees like that create.

Improving Retention

Perhaps even more difficult than *attracting* top talent and ensuring full engagement at the workplace is *keeping* those people on board. It's fairly easy to create the illusion of a great culture for outside observers. But if an organization's leaders don't truly care about people's well-being and their personal and professional growth, it won't take long for staff members to see right through the façade.

Keeping great employees on our team is also an extremely important competitive advantage. Talented people who do great work can easily find positions at other organizations, even in the toughest economy. There is a significant cost to losing them and having to replace them. In addition to the losses in the value these top performers bring, the HR costs alone should motivate us to reduce turnover as much as possible. When we factor in the costs of recruiting, interviews, lack of productivity during training, and so forth, the cost of turnover is generally estimated by HR professionals to be one year of salary for mid-level employees and as much as two to three years of salary for senior managers.

Considering these numbers, it is a very sound practice to invest in the training and programs—and the time to make the shift in your approach in leadership—that can help us develop a culture like the one at Next Jump. For example, imagine that you have a business that has 100 employees, that turnover is 13 percent (this was the average turnover rate calculated by the Society for Human Resource Management in 2011), and that the average salary is only $35,000. This means that turnover costs roughly $450,000 each year. Thus, if you invest $100,000 in creating a culture like the one at Next Jump and reduce turnover by only 6 percent, you would save $210,000 in reduced turnover costs. This would provide you with a 210 percent return on your investment.

If you can develop a culture like this, you would probably not have to worry too much about retention. Turnover at Next Jump is around 1 percent, whereas the industry average is 22 percent. This is true despite the fact that NxJumpers routinely get calls from other companies in the tech space offering them two to three times the pay they receive at Next Jump. Even two or three hundred thousand dollars per year of additional salary is not enough to entice them to leave their work family—a family that truly cares about them, serves them, and inspires them to achieve great things.

4 Creating a Highly Innovative Culture

Linking Innovation Directly to Profit

Dr. E. Ted Prince, founder of the prestigious Perth Leadership Institute, began his climb to the peaks of the leadership development world from one of the lowest of the proverbial valleys. Abandoned by his mother at a young age, he grew up in the harsh environment of an orphanage outside London, England, in the days when neglect and maltreatment were the norm. He had a brief respite from orphanage life as a teenager, when his mother returned to take custody of him again. But he would soon find out that she was just using him to get a free ticket to move to Australia as part of a program offered by the British Government at the time. She abandoned him again almost immediately upon arriving in Australia.

Dr. Prince worked his way through college in Australia, but not without challenges. At one point, he was told by one of the most respected eye doctors in Australia that he was going to go blind, likely because of all the lead he was exposed to in the orphanage. He prepared for months to live the rest of his life without sight and lost his scholarship as a result of the prognosis.

Miraculously, although his sight deteriorated for some time, he never went blind. His sight eventually returned to normal. Despite the good news, Dr. Prince could not get his scholarship back, which meant he would have to take on another job to pay his way through school.

After graduating college, Dr. Prince went on to work for the Australian Social Security Administration (SSA). His seniors at the SSA recognized that he was both highly intelligent and very innovative, so he was quickly moved to a special position as part of a think tank. A short time after that, and only a few years out of college, he was promoted to be the director of IT for the entire Australian SSA, and he was credited for spearheading the organization's transition from paper to digital systems.

With this feat of leadership under his belt, Dr. Prince would move on to the corporate world. He served as the CEO of numerous firms throughout his career, including a publicly traded company. He also served on several corporate boards and earned a PhD in political science in his spare time.

The first time I met Dr. Prince was at his house. I was invited by a mutual friend of ours, a CEO of a large local company, to attend a mentoring session they led for a group of international students who were interested in entrepreneurship. Although I knew almost nothing of Dr. Prince's background at the time, it became very clear as he answered our questions that his life experiences had made him very wise. Since I was just starting out on the leadership development work I was doing, I was looking for mentors to help me develop. I decided almost immediately that Dr. Prince would be an excellent mentor for me. I made it a point to speak with him one-on-one later and ask if we could meet for lunch. He was glad to meet.

At our lunch meeting, I began by asking him to explain a little more about how he got his start doing leadership consulting, which turned out to be an intriguing story. When Dr. Prince retired, he wanted to continue his work. He is a very creative person and without an outlet of some type, he told me he probably would have driven himself crazy. So, he started doing some leadership development consulting work with CEOs that he knew, essentially as a hobby. After spending a good deal of time consulting, he realized that there wasn't really any leadership training for improving a leader's business acumen—generally defined as the ability to understand and deal with a business situation in a way that results in a positive outcome—in a precise way. The training available seemed pretty subjective to him, with no concrete methods for linking leadership to the bottom line.

Dr. Prince started looking for research that focused on measuring and developing a manager's ability to create capital. After an exhaustive search, he discovered that although there are myriad behavioral assessments used for leadership development, none of them can be linked directly to financial outcomes. Apparently no one had ever done research that could directly link behavioral traits to the bottom line.

Dr. Prince did what any innovative entrepreneur would do: He decided to research the link between leadership behaviors and profitability. He founded the Perth Leadership Institute and, over a period of about 10 years, spent well over $1 million conducting extensive, rigorous research involving hundreds of business executives. His research has been published in several highly regarded journals, as well as in a book entitled *The Three Financial Styles of Very Successful Leaders* (McGraw-Hill, 2005).[1]

The result of Dr. Prince's research is a leadership development program called the Perth Leadership Outcome Model (PLOM), which includes personality assessments that can measure with great accuracy whether an individual member will add value to the organization. Specifically, the assessments measure the impact that a manager will have on gross margin and expenses. Based on the assessments, the PLOM then offers research-based ideas and tools for helping people who are not behaving in profitable ways to change their behavior so that they can begin to positively impact the bottom line.

Dr. Prince made a great discovery in his research: The impact a manager will have on gross margin and expenses is a result of behaviors that are usually unconscious, and are the effects of what are known as *cognitive biases*. These biases are habitual tendencies, usually resulting in a divergence from optimum results, that are reflected in reasoning, evaluating, remembering, or other cognitive processes. They cause us to hold on to our preferences and beliefs regardless of contrary information. They also cause us to unconsciously filter out information that might be very important.

A now-famous example of a temporary bias that the brain creates is seen in an experiment that has participants watch a video showing six people—three with white shirts and three with black—passing a basketball around. Participants were asked to count how many times the three people in white shirts pass the ball during the brief video. About halfway through, a person dressed in a gorilla costume enters the screen from the right, breakdances through the action, and exits to the left.

After the video was finished, participants were asked to state how many times the white team passed the ball, and if they noticed anything other than six people passing basketballs in the video. If they claimed they hadn't seen anything other than the people passing basketballs, they were asked whether they saw anything unusual happen during the video. If they said they did not see anything unusual, they were asked something like, "Did you notice the gorilla breakdance through the action?"

Incredibly, nearly half of the participants completely missed the dancing gorilla. These people were the victims of a temporary cognitive bias created by their brain. Because they were so focused on counting the passes, their brain had made them blind to the fact that there was a dancing gorilla in the video. In fact, they were so convinced that there was no way there could have been a dancing gorilla passing through the action, they demanded to see the video again. Of course, it was very obvious when one was looking for it.[2]

Although this example involves a temporary bias, most cognitive biases are long-lasting and can persist an entire lifetime without some type of intervention. An example of the effects of more permanent cognitive biases are what happens in jury trials. People serving on juries are often unable to ignore irrelevant features of the case, weigh the relevant features appropriately, consider different possibilities open-mindedly, and resist fallacies such as appeals to emotion. Each one of these errors is due to cognitive biases. In fact, because psychologists can measure the cognitive biases, they are actually able to predict quite accurately which jurors will fail and in what ways.[3]

Although we may not want to admit it, we all have numerous types of cognitive biases. They act as filters that affect how we perceive and respond to the world around us. We make many decisions that are affected by these cognitive biases, which in most cases are *unconscious*—that is, we are completely unaware we even have them. Unfortunately, most of these cognitive biases result in adverse personal, professional, and financial outcomes. For instance, we may make 15 decisions per day that have negative impacts—small or large—on gross margin and expenses, simply because we are unaware of the cognitive biases that influenced the decisions.

Armed with the simple understanding of how cognitive biases affect decisions, Dr. Prince has been able to do some amazing things with his research. Most relevant to the discussion here, he was able to identify the cognitive biases that lead to either positive or negative financial outcomes. One of the most interesting findings in this part of the research is that only a small minority of people are naturally hardwired to be profitable over time. This explains why the vast majority of businesses go through the business life cycle—growing, reaching a plateau, and eventually declining and going out of business altogether.

Dr. Prince identified 10 cognitive biases that have significant, direct impacts on gross margin and expenses. There are two in particular that his research shows have the greatest impact on the bottom line. One of them is the *illusion of control* bias. This bias results in an exaggerated estimation of how much control we have over events. In the business world this results in a strong tendency to act based on the belief that applying more resources to a potential solution will result in a more positive outcome. The stronger this bias is in a person, the more likely he is to consume more resources to achieve a desired result.

Of course, the more it costs to achieve a result, the less profitable that course of action will be. If we can achieve a result for $10, without compromising our values, why would we spend $15? A person with a strong illusion of control bias will often spend the extra $5 and fully believe that the extra cost would improve the outcome. This person would be decreasing the profitability of an organization with every decision he makes. And, the higher up in leadership this person is, the greater the impact on the organization. Imagine the effects of someone who consistently spends $1.5 million to achieve a result than only requires $1 million.

The second of the two cognitive biases with the greatest impact on profitability, the *status quo bias*, is most relevant to the topic of innovation. This bias is an excellent predictor of whether or not a person will be innovative. The Perth Leadership Institute's research shows very clearly that innovation has a tremendous impact on gross margin. In fact, we can predict quite accurately how a manager will affect gross margin simply by measuring how innovative that manager is.

This makes perfect sense; there is a direct correlation between how unique a product or service is and the price someone is willing to pay for it. Thus, the more innovative someone is, the more likely she is to create products and services that add value for the consumer, which also increases the profit margin for the organization offering the product or service. This is also true when the end consumer is our own organization. A person who offers innovative solutions internal to the organization can help create a significant competitive advantage that results in added value.

What Does Being Innovative *Actually* Mean?

Innovation is a common buzzword these days. Yet, there doesn't seem to be a lot of clarity on what exactly innovation is. Returning to the discussion on the status quo bias will help shed some light on what it actually means to be an innovator.

The status quo bias, which is based on our need to fit in, results in a strong preference for maintaining things the way they have been. As you might guess, most people have at least a moderately strong status quo bias. The need for belonging is one of the most powerful human needs, and doing things that buck the status quo makes most people feel as though they're risking others' acceptance. Unfortunately, the stronger this bias is in a person, the less likely he is to come up with innovative solutions to problems that add value to the organization or for customers.

People with little or no status quo bias tend to be more innovative in their thinking. These people have no problem suggesting and acting on ideas that are completely outside of the proverbial box, even if the majority of people reject that idea as "silly" over long periods of time. In others words, people with little or no status quo bias typically don't care what other people think about them or their ideas. Often times, people like this are difficult to get along with.

Although Dr. Prince is not one of those people who are difficult to get along with, he is very innovative. His research helped him understand why. Our biases are formed while we're growing up—a period during which Dr. Prince never experienced *normalcy*. The only constants in his life were continuous change and unpleasant situations that he hoped would change. His life was the antithesis of the status quo, so there was never a chance for a status quo bias to develop.

You might have noticed that creativity was not metioned in the above description of what makes a person innovative. Perhaps the most common misperception about innovation is that it is synonymous with creativity. Although creativity can assist in innovating, it is certainly not necessary. In fact, there is research showing that people who tend to be very creative are actually unlikely to innovate, because innovation has a lot more to do with execution than it does with creativity. Someone who has too many ideas often lacks the focus to stick with one long enough to create the disruption in the field or marketplace that we refer to as an *innovation*. The most important element of being innovative is the ability to stay with an idea long enough, even in the face of significant opposition, to actually make the idea a reality and have at least a small group of people adopt it.

A good example of this is Bill Gates, who is widely regarded as one of the most innovative people of our time. Gates did not create DOS, which was the foundation on which Microsoft was built. Rather, he bought it from people who were likely much more creative than him. But those people weren't innovators. They didn't have the vision and the courage to stick with their idea for years, despite having no real market for it, until the market emerged around their idea. But Bill Gates did, and that's what makes him an innovator.

Building a Highly Innovative Culture

Prior to when I became a trainer with the Perth Leadership Institute, Dr. Prince and his team had designed an entire program to identify the people within an organization that had high potential as innovators and to help the leaders better understand how to work with them. The program was created because the research conducted by Dr. Prince shows that highly innovative people can add a tremendous amount of value to an organization, and that they are also rather rare and often quite challenging to work with. People with little or no status quo bias often don't like to follow rules or don't have the best people skills. These people generally are less inclined to be service oriented and tend not to work well in a team setting.

Because of the skill required to work with highly innovative people, organizations that have such people on their teams often find it quite difficult to keep them on the team. This is especially true for large organizations. Nothing will drive away highly innovative people more quickly than high levels of bureaucracy. Most large organizations become increasingly bureaucratic as they grow. As a result, they drive away innovators and gradually become less innovative as an organization overall.

There are, of course, exceptions to this general trend. It is possible, even in large companies, to create a culture that attracts and retains highly innovative people and, perhaps more impor-tant, helps people who are not naturally very innovative (the vast majority of people) to be more innovative. Creating such a culture is rather easy when we have leaders who are devoted to serving and caring for people.

An example of this is the networking giant Cisco Systems.[4] In 2012, Cisco posted revenues of nearly $50 billion and employed over 70,000 people. Yet, despite their size, Cisco is known for being one of the most innovative companies in the world.

In April of 2012, I met Padmasree Warrior, the chief tech-nology and strategy officer for Cisco. Mrs. Warrior is in charge of roughly 30,000 engineers, and she is clearly an expert on skillfully leading highly innovative people. I saw her speak earlier in the year at the Wisdom 2.0 conference in San Francisco, and it appeared as though she really strives to serve the members of her team and take good care of them. When I had the chance to speak with her one-on-one, she told me that she thinks it's extremely important for leaders to apply the principles of servant leadership in order to create and maintain a highly innovative culture.

Many other highly innovative large companies seem to take the same view. Two excellent examples are Google[5] and software giant SAS,[6] which are among the most innovative companies in the world. Every year, these two companies are also both highly ranked among best companies for which to work. In fact, they were listed as number one and two on *Fortune* magazine's 2013 list.

The examples of how Google works to care for employees are almost legendary. They include free, on-site haircuts; gyms; pools; break rooms with video games, ping-pong, billiards, and foosball; on-site medical staff for easy doctor appointments; and the option to bring one's dog in to work.

But Google didn't invent this type of incredible workplace culture. They actually emulated the culture at SAS, a company that has produced absolutely phenomenal business outcomes. SAS has posted record earnings for 37 consecutive years, including $2.8 billion in 2012. CEO Jim Goodnight often says that the secret to their success is taking care of employees.

SAS has many perks similar to those at Google, including unlimited sick days; on-site childcare valued at $410 per month, which makes it possible for parents to have lunch with their kids; summer camp for kids; car cleaning; a beauty salon; a state-of-the-art, 66,000-square-foot gym; and a free on-site health care clinic, staffed by physicians, nutritionists, physical therapists, and psychologists.

Why Serving and Caring for People Results in a Highly Innovative Culture

There are many organizations that don't have the budgets to provide the perks offered at Google and SAS. Fortunately, the perks aren't necessary. What's most important is consistently and authentically caring for the people on our teams. When we truly care about team members and are committed to helping them grow, we don't stifle innovation by worrying about our own positions. Instead of feeling as though *we* have to come up with all the ideas to look good as leaders, we are happy when our teams have great ideas. Leaders who primarily focus on their own performance—instead of on how well they lead people—tend to micromanage, which erodes trust and crushes innovation.

Another reason serving and caring for the people on our team helps to build and sustain an innovative culture is that leaders who care about the people around them are much better at modeling and teaching empathy. Being able to empathize with others can be essential in determining what they might need and how we can solve their problems. People with high levels of empathy are much more likely to see a need that our customers might have, and thereby add value for our customers by meeting that need, whether it's simply a matter of better customer service or an entirely new product or service that we can offer.

Having empathy can also be extremely helpful in the process of advancing a new idea. As previously discussed, the most important element of innovation is the ability to execute on an idea. Unless we are in a one-person company, this means that we often need others' support to be able to move our ideas forward. We need to be able to understand other people's points of view and discern their motivations. According to a study published in the *Harvard Business Review*, this ability to understand others' motivations and craft a message that addresses their needs is the most essential skill for people trying to innovate within an organization.[7]

When we truly care about and are committed to helping people grow, we are also much more likely to trust them with higher levels of autonomy. This is one of the most important elements of attracting and retaining those rare, highly innovative people who abhor bureaucracy but can add so much value to our organizations. This is why both Google and SAS give employees a tremendous amount of freedom in the hours they work. Employees at SAS essentially create their own schedules, which allows them to plan work around important events.

Serving and caring for team members can also help those who are not naturally innovative become more innovative. In some cases, focusing on this strategy might be a better course of action because highly innovative people are generally not likely to be a good fit for a culture devoted to serving others (although they, too, can be trained to develop a more service-oriented mentality)—and they are very rare. As discussed earlier, most people have a fairly strong status quo bias, making it very unlikely that they'll suggest and act on ideas that are contrary to the status quo—that is, ideas that are innovative. Their fears of rejection and not fitting in—and, in the case of the business world, of being fired—hold them back in this regard.

When we are focused on serving team members and consistently caring for them, we can alleviate those fears. With consistent care, people trust us more, and they know that we will not fire them for taking appropriate risks and making mistakes. The more secure people feel, the more likely they are to suggest and act on innovative ideas. We are essentially removing the status quo bias by removing the status quo.

Jim Goodnight of SAS offers a great example of just how powerful this can be. In the fall of 2008, the Great Recession was imminent. SAS faced the same issues that every other company in the analytics software industry faced. Sales plunged and almost every business was making budget cuts in preparation for what seemed like a long downturn. Many companies in almost every industry started laying off large numbers of employees to make their numbers work, so SAS employees began to fear that the same thing would happen at their company.

But Goodnight's response to the recession was dramatically different, as Mark C. Crowley, author of *Lead From the Heart: Transformational Leadership for the 21st Century*, describes in an article he wrote for *Fast Company*:

> In early January 2009, Goodnight held a global webcast and announced that none of its 13,000 worldwide employees would lose their job. He simply asked them all to be vigilant with spending and to help the firm endure the storm. "By making it very clear that no one was going to be laid off," Goodnight told me, "suddenly we cut out huge amounts of chatter, concern, and worry—and people got back to work."[8]

At the time, SAS had a 33-year streak of record revenues. Jim Goodnight was perfectly willing to let that record go to make sure that people felt safe. He knew that by caring for team members and ensuring that they felt safe, he would be creating the space for continued innovation. As a result of his care, employees at SAS did continue to disrupt the market with innovations and the company had another record year while everyone else struggled just to stay alive.

5 Delivering World-Class Customer Service

In 1995, Nick Swinmurn graduated from of the University of California, Santa Barbara, with a degree in film studies. For several years after graduation, he bounced around between several jobs and, in 1999, ended up doing contract work for a tech company in the San Francisco Bay Area. One day that year, Nick was looking for shoes at the mall in the city. He found shoes that were the right style, but not the right color. He then found shoes with the right color, but not the right size. After an hour of searching without success, Nick went home to try his luck on the Internet.

Nick's online search was also unsuccessful. The only people selling shoes online were a couple of "mom and pop" stores that had very small selections from which to choose. It was at this point that Nick had a revelation of sorts. He realized that at this time, at the onset of the Internet boom, no major online retailers were specializing in selling shoes, and he recognized a tremendous opportunity. His idea was to create an online store that offered the absolute best selection in shoes. The store would have the most brands, styles, colors, sizes, and widths, so that people could always find the perfect shoe within a few minutes. He thought he had stumbled upon pure gold!

Unfortunately, no one else saw it that way. Everyone he told about his idea replied by telling Nick that he was crazy. "People, especially women, will never be comfortable buying shoes online," they said. And they were right—almost.

With the help of the great visionary entrepreneur Tony Hsieh, Nick's idea eventually became the online shoe retailing giant that we know today as Zappos.com. In less than 10 years, Zappos.com grew from essentially zero sales to $1 billion in sales. In November 2009, Amazon.com acquired Zappos in a deal valued at $1.2 billion. What Nick's naysayers didn't consider was the one element of the business model that would be required for it to work: delivering absolutely unprecedented customer service.

The only way people would be comfortable buying shoes online is if the process was essentially identical to buying shoes in the store. And the only way to make that happen was to ship the shoes extremely quickly and allow them to try the shoes on free of risk, just as they can in the store. This meant that Zappos.com would have to allow people to return the shoes, no questions asked, and that they would have to pay for the shipping.

So that's what they did.

Out of necessity, Zappos.com started out with an extreme customer focus. This evolutionary requirement, if you will, turned out to be an incredible asset; it laid the foundation for how the culture at Zappos.com would grow. "Deliver WOW through service," is the first core value of the company, so "wowing" the customer with amazing service has become the basis for almost every decision the leaders make at Zappos.com.

Unlike most customer service call centers for U.S. firms, the Zappos.com call center is full of real human beings. The company is extremely committed to ensuring that those human beings are passionate about having a job with the primary objective of wowing the customers, and that they are capable of actually doing it. Many people are aware of Zappos' approach to training: After potential employees have completed about a week of the intensive customer service training, they are offered $2,000 to quit if they don't think that Zappos.com is the right place for them. Zappos' leaders know that anyone who would take the offer is not committed enough to wowing customers, and would cost the company much more than $2,000 over time as a result of customers not having an absolutely amazing experience when dealing with the company.

The employees that stay are committed to wowing customers, and they go through weeks of intensive training to learn how to better do that. They are also allowed to spend as much time on an inbound phone call as they like. In fact, they are told that they're expected to take as much time as they need to ensure each customer has an amazing experience.

Most call centers incentivize customer service reps to handle as many calls as possible during a day as a way to reduce costs—an approach that Zappos' leaders see as a very bad one. It essentially guarantees that most customers will receive average customer service, at best. Zappos.com recognizes that, in the long run, it's much better for the bottom line to give reps the freedom to spend as much time as they need to with each customer, even if the conversation has little or nothing to do with buying something from Zappos.com.

In fact, according to a great article published in the *Huffington Post*,[1] on December 8, 2012, a rep at Zappos.com set a record for the company by spending 10 hours and 29 minutes on a phone call with a customer talking mostly about things other than clothing and shoes. Although most managers would see a call like this as a waste of time, Zappos.com sees it as a great marketing investment. It probably only cost Zappos.com a few hundred dollars for the employee to spend 10 hours on the phone. The story of that call was reported in a slew of other media—the *Digital Journal, The Consumerist, Global Post, Business Insider*, and many others. Millions of people heard about the call from highly credible sources. How many companies do you suppose have media reporting on their customer service calls? It happens regularly for Zappos.com.

But Zappos.com goes beyond encouraging long, highly personalized customer phone calls. Their reps are known for going above and beyond the call of duty in their efforts to wow. In March of 2011, a customer service rep physically went to a rival shoe store to get a specific pair of shoes for a woman staying at a hotel in Las Vegas because Zappos.com had run out of stock. That year, another rep learned about a best man who had forgotten to pack his dress shoes. The rep sent a pair of shoes overnight, for free, to ensure that the man would enjoy the big day.

One customer's mother had recently undergone medical treatment that left her feet numb and sensitive to pressure, which made most of her shoes useless. The customer ordered six pairs of shoes for her mother from Zappos.com, hoping that at least one of them would work. After receiving the shoes, her mother called Zappos.com to get instructions on how to return the shoes that didn't work, and she explained why she was returning so many shoes. Two days later, the woman received a large bouquet of flowers from Zappos.com, which included a nice note wishing her well and that she would recover from her treatments soon. Two days later, the customer, her mother, and her sister were all upgraded to Zappos.com "VIP Member" status, which gives them all free expedited shipping on all orders.

Quantifying the ROI in Customer Service

Most people intuitively know that delivering excellent customer service is one the most important elements of running a successful organization. Clearly, we would much rather have happy, loyal customers than dissatisfied *former* customers who tell others how terrible our organization is. We know that improved customer service results in happier, more loyal customers, which is great for earning repeat business and earning more customer referrals. However, there are very few organizations that treat their customers with a level of care that is even close to the level of care that Zappos' customers experience. Why do you suppose this is?

One reason could be that leaders simply haven't seen data that quantifies the return on capital invested in delivering high levels of customer service. If we can't see how an investment is likely to create a great return for our organization, it would clearly be an unsound practice to make such an investment. Fortunately, there is now a good deal of research showing the quantifiable benefits of investing in improved customer service.

One area that has received a lot of attention is the tremendous competitive advantage of *retaining customers*. Depending on how we account for costs, different studies show that businesses spend between five and seven times more on recruiting a new customer than they do on retaining existing customers. The reason we see these returns of 500 to 700 percent on capital invested in retaining customers is not just because we spend more on marketing to acquire new customers than we spend on keeping our current customers happy. It turns out that service is significantly more important than price for current customers.

According to the Fourth Annual Study on Customer Service for the United States, conducted by Accenture,[2] 73 percent of customers reported that they left a service provider because of poor customer service, while only 47 percent left because of a lower price. Current, satisfied customers are willing to pay a premium for the value they receive from great service, so they are much less sensitive to price than are new customers. Thus, a company that delivers exceptional customer service will be able to consistently and safely realize higher margins than their competitors. For example, American Express once surveyed its customers and found that most would be willing to spend an average of an extra 9 percent with a company that provided exceptional customer service![3]

Another study by Downton, Rustema, and Van Veen—funded by Oracle and conducted over a three-year period—showed that high levels of customer service were linked to several improved business outcomes. The research showed that companies that trained sales reps to focus more on customer service, which allowed them to be seen more as "trusted advisors," realized an average increase in sales of 20 percent. Companies that effectively made improvements in the customer experience, which led to just a 5 percent increase in customer loyalty, consistently realized profit increases from 25 to 85 percent. The successful service initiatives also consistently resulted in productivity improvements, which in turn resulted in increases in both gross and net margins.[4]

Some of the most compelling research comes from an excellent experiment reported by the Database Marketing Institute.[5] A building products manufacturer and a consulting firm ran an experiment wherein they divided their top 1,200 customers into a test group of 600 and a control group of 600. They treated the control group exactly as they'd treated all other customers in the past, but they significantly ramped up communication with decision makers in the test group. They did not try to sell. They did not offer discounts. They simply worked at deepening friendships and providing valuable information—and they achieved impressive results.

After six months, the test group made 12 percent more orders than they had in the previous six months, while the control group actually made 18 percent fewer orders (likely because of the recession). The test group placed 14 percent larger orders, while orders the control group placed were actually 14 percent smaller than before. Overall, the test group ended up spending $2.6 million more with the company than did the control group during the test period. The test only cost $50,000, so the return on investment over six months was 5,200 percent.

How Great Leaders Inspire World-Class Customer Service

A thought-provoking article on CBSNews.com[6] noted that the median annual compensation for CEOs of the public companies in the Customer Service Hall of Fame was a little over $3 million,

while the median annual compensation for CEOs of companies in the Customer Service Hall of Shame was a whopping
$14.9 million. This data suggests that there may be a correlation
between selfish senior leaders and poor customer service. I
cite this merely to emphasize the importance of having great
leadership if we want to offer great customer service. This may be
a more important factor in determining customer service levels
than the specific tactics that we employ, of which there are many.

There are numerous books written specifically about great
customer service tactics. (I've included some great examples on
the recommended reading list on my website.) But we must first
have great leadership for any of those tactics to be sustainable.
World-class customer service is simply a side effect when we lead
with a focus on serving others, and tactics appropriate for our
organization and our customers become a natural—and more
easily sustained—response.

In order to consistently deliver world-class customer service
and reap all of the benefits previously listed, our customers need
to feel sincerely cared for every single time they interact with
our organization, whether it's with a customer service rep or
an accountant. Every member of our organization should see
themselves as a customer service rep and be able to help the
customer—whether that's another member of our organization
or a person who uses our products or services—to feel sincerely
cared for. As Zappos.com CEO Tony Hseih has famously said,
"customer service shouldn't be just a department. It should be the
entire company."

This, of course, requires that we hire people who are not only
competent, but also capable of and willing to care for and serve
others. It also requires us, as leaders, to ensure that those people

are *happy* while they're at work. Unless they have extremely high levels of emotional intelligence, unhappy people will not be able to serve a customer in a way that leaves that customer feeling wowed and sincerely cared for.

How do we attract these kinds of people to our organizations—those who are willing and able to truly care for and serve others? And how do we then ensure that those people are happy and consistently able to deliver world-class customer service? It's simple—and it starts at the top. Leaders need to consistently deliver world-class customer service to our most important customers: the people on our team. We should be treating the people we lead with the exact same level of care that we expect them to deliver to the customer. If members of our team don't feel sincerely cared for, neither will our customers.

Leaders of organizations that offer world-class customer service know this. In fact, the leaders of many of the companies that are ranked highest in customer service, like Southwest Airlines and Zappos.com, state explicitly that the end consumer is *not* their number one priority—employees are. They know that a happy, loyal employee results in happy, loyal customers.

In addition to the anecdotal evidence, and the fact that this simply makes sense intuitively, there is also a growing body of research quantifying the relationship between employee satisfaction and customer satisfaction. Some of the research is rather broad. For example, there is a significant amount that links an organization's recognition as one of the "best companies to work for" to higher levels of customer satisfaction.

Some of the research is much more specific, including a study at Sears Roebuck & Co., which demonstrated that a 5 percent improvement in employee attitudes led to a 1.3 percent increase in customer satisfaction which, in turn, resulted in a 0.5 percent increase in revenues.[7] We wouldn't have to spend a dime to improve employee attitudes 5 or 10 percent. Just a little extra care could easily achieve that. That's a return on investment that is technically infinite.

Another study, conducted by Wiley and Brooks in 2000, found that depending on market segment and industry, between 40 and 80 percent of customer satisfaction and customer loyalty was linked directly to employee satisfaction.[8] In other words, in many of these cases, employee satisfaction was significantly more important for ensuring customer satisfaction than the product itself!

Developing Employees Who Wow Your Customers

There is another tremendous advantage of having unselfish leaders who are committed to serving and caring for employees. Because such leaders are always considering others' needs, they are much more likely to think of ways to empower employees and extend them high levels of trust. This is an extremely important element of delivering world-class customer service. Employees who are empowered to do whatever it takes to wow the customer are much more likely to do so than those who must get permission to do anything outside of the proverbial box.

One company that understands the power of this principle is Wegmans Food Markets, known for being the industry leader in customer service. Trust and empowerment are core values at Wegmans. The company's leaders allow employees to make decisions that can improve their work or benefit the customer. They know that when they place high levels of trust in employees and give them the freedom to wow the customer, the risk-reward ratio is very low. It's highly unlikely that an employee would do serious harm, but it is highly likely that an employee would care for customers in ways that can have tremendous, positive impacts on the company.

For example, one of Wegmans's customers had to miss a family reunion in another state because she could not get off from work. She called a Wegmans store near the location of the reunion and asked if she could order a cake and pay for it over the phone. Wegmans has a store policy that prohibits processing payments over the phone, but the employee did it anyway.

The customer e-mailed Wegmans and wrote, "I wanted you to be aware that today two people saw the humanity and importance of people, not policy. Thank you for allowing your associates to use their decision-making ability and common sense to assist me. The request may have been small, but it means the world to me to participate in a family celebration."

When we empower employees to make little decisions that can have big impacts, we develop people into leaders who can make big decisions with even bigger impacts, as the following story conveys. Unfortunately, this powerful example begins with some very sad circumstances.

In January of 2011, near Denver, Colorado, a two-year-old boy named Caden was beaten by his mother's live-in boyfriend. His injuries were so severe that he almost immediately went into a coma. Medical professionals determined the next day that Caden would not survive, and that he would be taken off of life support that night so that his organs could be donated and potentially help over 20 people.

Mark Dickinson, Caden's grandfather, was in Los Angeles on business when he received the tragic news. Mr. Dickinson's wife immediately arranged for him to fly to Denver, with a connection in Tucson, Arizona. She informed the carrier, Southwest Airlines, of the circumstances and let them know that her husband would be rushing to catch his flight in Los Angeles because, if he missed his connection, he wouldn't be able to see his grandson for the last time before the child was taken off of life support.

Mr. Dickinson arrived at LAX in what appeared to be plenty of time, almost two hours before the scheduled departure. But there were long lines at check in. By the time he got his boarding pass, he was already anxious that he might miss his flight. When he arrived at security, he noticed immediately that the lines were lengthy and moving very slowly.

Mr. Dickinson's anxiety escalated significantly as the reality began to sink in that he might miss his flight, along with the chance to see his grandson for the last time. He told security about his situation and asked if he could get to the front. They told him he would have to wait just like everyone else.

After going through security, Mr. Dickinson realized that he was already late. On the verge of tears, he grabbed his shoes and sprinted to his gate in his socks. He arrived at his gate 12 minutes late. His heart must have broken.

To his surprise, though, he was met at the gate by both the ticketing agent and the pilot. The ticketing agent said, "Are you Mark?"

"Yes," he replied.

"We held the plane for you and we're so sorry about the loss of your grandson."

Although this may seem like a small gesture, as James F. Parker points out in his book *Do The Right Thing*, Southwest has mastered the art of turning airplanes around quickly. On average, they turn their planes around 15 to 20 minutes faster than their competitors—something that saves Southwest approximately $3 billion per year. So for Southwest, 12 minutes is essentially an eternity. Making a habit out of holding airplanes for 12 extra minutes would cost the company hundreds of millions of dollars per year.

According to an article on Dailymail.com, as the pilot escorted Mr. Dickinson down the jetway, Mr. Dickinson said, "I can't thank you enough for this."

The pilot replied, "They can't go anywhere without me and I wasn't going anywhere without you. Now relax. We'll get you there. And, again, I'm so sorry."[9]

Little Caden was taken off of life support that night at 9:20 p.m. Thanks to the kindness and compassion of the pilot, and the leaders at Southwest who empowered him to make the call, Mark Dickinson was there to say goodbye.

When asked how the leaders at Southwest Airlines felt about the pilot's decision in an interview with AOL Travel News, Southwest spokeswoman Marilee McInnis stated that, "We fully support what our captain did. Customer service is important and we're not at all surprised an action like this would take place."[10]

The leaders at Southwest weren't upset with the pilot for holding the plane. They were *proud* of him—as they should be. Southwest is the airline that love built. And, because the company's leaders have effectively passed on their values and empowered employees to make important decisions on the spot, they helped ensure that the pilot valued being compassionate above short-term gain. In the long term, his decision will also likely result in numerous positive business outcomes. It was an incredible example of customer service that inspired everyone who saw it, was reported extensively in the media, and will be talked about for years to come, providing Southwest with a tremendous amount of free, highly impactful advertising.

6 Why Serving Others Is a Highly Effective Marketing Tactic

October 29, 2012, was not a typical Monday on the east coast of the United States by any stretch of the imagination. By 9:00 that morning, Hurricane Sandy made landfall just north of Atlantic City, New Jersey. The storm had enough power to wash away a 50-foot section of the Atlantic City boardwalk, and it devastated most of the New Jersey coastline. But the impact of the storm extended well beyond New Jersey.

Sandy was the largest Atlantic hurricane on record, with winds spanning roughly 1,100 miles and affecting states as far inland as Wisconsin. The storm resulted in almost $70 billion in damage, making it the second most costly storm in U.S. history, surpassed only by Hurricane Katrina. Sandy also resulted in the deaths of nearly 300 people in seven different countries.

The headquarters office for Next Jump is only 130 miles away from where Sandy made landfall in New Jersey. Although the Next Jump offices are located numerous floors up in the building, they were nevertheless rendered useless by the storm. New York governor Andrew Cuomo had declared a state of emergency three days earlier. All the major airports in the city shut down. The subways were sealed off to prevent them from being flooded and submerged as they had been during Hurricane Irene in 2011. By mid-morning that Monday, much of Manhattan had lost power, including the Flatiron district, where the Next Jump headquarters is located.

Although the New York office serves as their headquarters, Next Jump also has offices in Boston, San Francisco, and London. The Boston office quickly became the temporary command center for the company. The first task was to ensure that all of the NxJumpers in New York were okay. This wasn't easy because they couldn't even reach some team members—including CEO Charlie Kim—by cell phone.

Once they'd accounted for everyone, steps were taken to ensure that business continued to run as normal for their customers. NxJumpers in the Boston office quickly stepped up to fill the void left by the crippled New York office. People in every department volunteered to take on any role that was needed. The lead engineer became the interim head of the customer service team. A senior developer and an associate from the human capital team became customer service reps. The entire security engineering team worked around the clock to make sure disaster recovery procedures were underway. A NxJumper on an international vacation had heard about the storm and contacted the Boston office to ask how he could pitch in. To support the e-mail operations team in Boston, another engineer moved into her in-law's house so that she would have access to power. It seemed that every single person asked, "What can I do to help?"

Compared to other companies in New York, Next Jump was very fortunate to have multiple offices staffed with very talented, service-oriented people who could so seamlessly fill the gaps in Next Jump's operations. The NxJumpers in New York were also very fortunate. They were all salaried employees, so none of them lost any pay during their week away from work. However, thousands of employees from other New York businesses, who earned hourly wages, lost an entire week of pay.

Charlie pointed this out to team members when they came back to work the Monday following the storm, and NxJumpers responded with incredible compassion. They realized that if they each donated 10 percent of their next paycheck, they could collectively cover the loss of pay experienced by the hourly employees with whom they often interact. They started a fund for that purpose and began nominating people who would be candidates for receiving help. Within a few days, the list was rather long, and a large number of NxJumpers had donated a portion of their paychecks to support the effort.

In Figure 6.1, a NxJumper named Lokeya is shown handing an envelope filled with enough money to cover a week of pay for two hourly employees at the local Dunkin' Donuts. Lokeya stated, "I mentioned to them that my company's employees had put this together. When I explained the details and told them that there was money in this envelope and my company wants to help, they were so happy and said 'Oh my God' at least 10 to 15 times."

Employees at Next Jump are hired in large part because of their capacity to serve and care for others, and leaders at Next Jump offer numerous ways to further develop that capacity. One example of how they're doing this is a program they began in late spring of 2013 called Adopt a Charity. Next Jump adopted

Figure 6.1

a charity called Summer Search, which helps severely under-privileged youth get long-term, highly committed mentoring that dramatically improves their chances of getting into and graduating from college. Charlie wrote the following in an e-mail to his NxJumpers explaining what they'd be giving to Summer Search: "[By letting them use our space] we are doubling their office space from 4,000 square feet to 10,000 square feet (half the eighth floor). We are taking their $200,000 in annual rent to $1 in annual rent."

In addition to use of the space, the Summer Search staff will have access to all of the amazing benefits offered at Next Jump, which is equivalent to about a 50 percent increase in their annual salaries. Also, NxJumpers will mentor both the staff and the youth with whom they work. Thus, NxJumpers not only get to see their leaders offer a great example of service to others, they will personally be afforded an opportunity to enjoy serving the Summer Search staff as well.

Another example of how the leaders at Next Jump encourage team members to serve is a program called Code for a Cause (CFAC). As mentioned in Chapter 3, Next Jump is able to attract and retain some of the most talented code writers in the world. The organization's leaders strongly encourage these brilliant individuals to spend at least two weeks each year away from Next Jump writing code for any NPO they would like to help out—and they are paid their full salary to do so.

The results of the program are amazing. NxJumpers go out in teams of three and often complete in 10 days projects that some NPOs have been trying to get done for years. After helping with the various NPOs, the NxJumpers come back to the office feeling like rock stars—inspired to help *other* NxJumpers become the best they can be and to use their talents to go out and serve others.

One example of a CFAC project is the work NxJumpers Henry, Akshit, and Awais did for the Incentive Mentoring Program (IMP) in the spring of 2013. Henry describes the program and their project in a blog post he wrote:

> IMP runs an eight-year program [through which they mentor] students from ninth grade through their senior year in college.... They provide daily car rides to school so the kids don't end up skipping school to join gangs. [They] spend hours in a library hashing out a college essay so that the kid is the first in her family to attend college. They volunteer ... to build houses [together to teach the kids] to think beyond themselves....
>
> IMP does amazing work with students, but unfortunately, 90 percent of the 40,000 hours that mentors put in last year

were undocumented. That's 36,000 hours spent with kids that were not recorded—which is painful for several reasons. One, the undocumented histories would be valuable to new mentors starting to work with a kid for the first time. Two, there's no way to give feedback to mentors. You can't applaud peers for a job well done, [or] provide guidance if they're having trouble. Three, it's a logistical nightmare trying to get all mentors to log their hours and manage all of it in pages and pages of spreadsheets.

Our team swooped in for two weeks and pumped out a product that solved these three pain points. The product allows mentors to log their activities, even from the convenience of a mobile device. It makes it a bit more fun to log because you can like and comment on posts. Lastly, mentor hours are recorded down to the very last minute, which makes it much easier to analyze all the hours invested at the end of the year. Our contact, the COO of IMP, described the product as a "game changer" and something that would "help us get to the next level." It was just an amazing feeling to hear that.[1]

Whereas many companies might see such a program as only a cost, the leaders at Next Jump see CFAC as a great investment. Among other benefits, they've found that CFAC is a great way to help their NxJumpers develop new skills in real-world situations. Their time on the IMP project allowed Henry, Akshit, and Awais to learn how to work with mobile frameworks and libraries, and gave them experience with project management and engaging with external clients.

These examples also highlight two more significant benefits to creating a culture devoted to serving and caring for others, like the culture at Next Jump. First, when people see that their peers and managers value their service to others, they tend to be much better team players. They think much less in terms of "what's in this for me" and "look at how great I am." Instead, they think in terms of "we." This is why NxJumpers function so well in teams. They frequently extend themselves to selflessly help other members of their team, as they did when Hurricane Sandy crippled New York.

But this spirit of serving and caring for others is universal in nature. It doesn't end where we encounter the borders defining our team. When we value and nurture this spirit of service, it gradually starts to expand quite naturally to include anyone we encounter who is in need of help, as we saw when NxJumpers gave up a portion of their salaries to help the hourly workers with whom they interact.

But why should we care about whether or not members of our team serve others outside of our organization? Isn't our goal to be highly effective leaders who help *our* organizations achieve greater success? Well, helping team members develop a spirit of service to the community can help us achieve that goal.

A company that's known for serving and caring for the community around it is a company that is more likely to attract the right kind of highly talented people who are essential for achieving success. And employees are much more likely to be fully engaged when they're proud of their organization and inspired by its virtuous behavior. Furthermore, those talented, highly engaged people are much more likely to *stay*. All of this has a huge impact on the bottom line.

Another benefit of creating this type of culture is that it can significantly strengthen our brand and result in an abundance of free, highly impactful, word-of-mouth advertising.

The well-known T-shirt company, Life is good,[2] is a great example of how powerful this benefit can be.

Smarter, More Enjoyable Marketing

In early October 2012, I heard Bert Jacobs, who co-founded the clothing brand Life is good with his brother John, tell the story of how their company has grown from start-up to $100 million in annual revenues. It definitely didn't get off to a fast start. In 1989, as John was finishing college and Bert was selling pizzas and teaching skating, the brothers decided to start selling T-shirts as a way to share their artwork. They started on the streets of Boston, and then moved on to door-to-door sales in college dorm rooms.

Although they didn't sell very many T-shirts, they were very frugal, so they eventually saved up enough money to buy an old minivan, which would allow them to sell to college dorms up and down the East Coast. To save money, they lived off of peanut butter and jelly sandwiches and slept in their van. They would travel for about six weeks at a time with one design, then return to Boston and throw a keg party to share highlights of their trip with their friends and brainstorm new design ideas. The brothers operated like this for about five years, barely scraping by.

On one of their trips between colleges, which could often last over four hours, Bert and John got into a deep discussion on how the media tends to focus on what's wrong with the world. They concluded that although catering to people's fears certainly sells, people were probably hungry for more optimism in life. They wondered if they could create a symbolic hero who inspired such optimism.

Based on that conversation, John drew the first image of Jake, which you've probably seen on a piece of Life is good apparel. John gave Jake a beret, which was meant to show that he was open-minded, and added shades to make him cool. And, of course, he drew the smile to show that Jake always finds a reason to be happy.

When the brothers showed the image of Jake at their next brainstorming keg party, people raved about it. One person commented, "This guy's got life figured out." Bert and John eventually condensed that idea down to "Life is good." They immediately printed up 48 Jake shirts to sell at a street fair in Cambridge, Massachusetts, the next day. They sold every shirt in 45 minutes flat, and knew they were on to something.

Within a short time, the brothers started selling the Jake shirts to retailers, who loved the idea and actually started to help Jake evolve as a character. The first retailer they approached was a small, mom-and-pop-type store whose owners asked Bert, "Does Jake eat ice cream?" Bert replied, "He will if you place an order!"

Other retailers asked if Jake likes to ride bikes or go hiking and fishing. Lo and behold, if the retailer placed an order, it turned out that Jake *did* like those things. This open-minded approach allowed the brothers to gradually expand their brand and their reach.

Jake T-shirts were wildly successful, and Bert and John were selling a lot of them. But, as Bert explains, they were so bad at the business side of things that it took them a few more years before they finally started making a profit. Once that happened, they hired a few "business-minded" people to help them run daily operations so they could focus on the big picture. They also hired a team of consultants to help them grow. The first thing the consultants said was, "You guys haven't done any advertising. You need to spend some money on advertising if you want to grow."

So, in 1999, the brothers put aside some money to run a test ad campaign, and started looking at options. Just when they were getting ready to invest in their first campaign, they saw an 11-year-old girl on the local news named Lindsey Beggan who immediately caught their attention. Lindsey had been diagnosed with a rare bone cancer. Some of the best doctors in world told her that they wouldn't be able to treat the cancer and that she would only live for about one more year. Bert and John noticed that while she was being interviewed, she wore a Life is good hat.

The reporter asked her why she wore Life is good apparel. After all, she had just been told she had less than a year to live. Lindsey replied that before she got sick, she took her life for granted. Now that she knew she only had a short time to live, she wanted to make sure that she appreciated every moment. The Life is good apparel reminded her of that.

Bert and John were deeply moved by Lindsey's story. They realized that their brand could make a significant impact on people, and they wanted to support that type of inspiration. They decided to take their advertising budget and spend it on creating a festival that would raise money to help Lindsey and other kids like her who face really serious challenges in life. The festival was wildly successful. The brothers raised a good deal of money for a good cause and, as a side effect, they received so much media and word-of-mouth exposure that they determined their return on investment from the festival was better than what they expected to earn from a traditional advertising campaign.

Marketing with the Spirit of Service

Years ago, the world of marketing underwent a sea change; *push marketing*—the traditional approach of attempting to influence people with unsolicited advertising messages through mass media—was on the verge of extinction. Nowadays, it's nearly impossible to find any marketing professional that doesn't stress the importance of *pull marketing*, a strategy centered on finding skillful ways to help people, earn their trust, and allow them to approach you when they're ready to purchase products or services.

Gary Vaynerchuck, a well-known and colorful thought leader in the world of marketing, gave a speech at an Inc. 500 conference in 2011 in which he explained quite clearly why businesses won't survive if they don't transition to increasing amounts of pull marketing. He asked the group of nearly 1,000 CEOs of the fastest-growing privately held companies in the country how many of them recorded their television programs. The majority of people raised their hands. He then asked how many people skip the commercials when they watch the recording. Almost everyone kept their hand up. He then asked the very pointed question: Why would we spend money on advertising that no one is watching?

Gary made another, equally eye-opening point: Imagine for a moment the vast amount of content—books, poems, movies, news articles, magazine articles, blog posts, and so on—that humanity has produced from the beginning of time until the year 2003. Today, according to Gary, humanity is now producing that same quantity of content every 48 hours. We are literally being bombarded with information.[3]

In this information age, in which we are exposed to more content in a few hours than the average person 1,000 years ago was exposed to in their entire lifetime, it's very, very difficult to gain and sustain a person's attention. Trying to do so by sending unsolicited messages requesting that people purchase our products or services is an exercise in futility, which is why most marketing experts are encouraging organizations to focus more on social media. Even Coca-Cola, perhaps the world's strongest and most recognizable brand, has realized that they need to focus more and more energy on their social media efforts. The company has invested in numerous, large, social media campaigns and has devoted a large number of staff to monitor and respond to these conversations.

It seems that the key to effective marketing in today's environment is to offer free content that is so valuable to people they want to share it with their friends, either in person or via social media. We are much more likely to take a look at something that our friends share with us than an unsolicited advertisement. One approach is to offer very helpful information for free that a customer might have had to pay for in the past. Content like this is something that people are likely to share, and that will simultaneously help people trust an organization and encourage them to learn more about what that organization does. This approach, commonly referred to as *content marketing*, is now taught by most marketing experts.

But there is an even more powerful approach to helping large numbers of people hear about our organizations, to quickly develop trust with us, and to spark the curiosity to learn more about us that often results in a new customer. That approach is to serve the community that our customers call home.

Some very interesting things start happening when we consistently serve our communities. First, because examples of companies that serve their communities in big ways are still relatively rare, they are newsworthy. This means that a company can often receive free exposure for their brand through the media, which has a much greater impact on people than an ad that is created to tell consumers about products or services.

People also love to share inspiring stories with their networks through social media. Acts of service and compassion can be spread quickly across large social networks, often times going "viral." One of my favorite examples is a video about a girl named Rachel.

Rachel donated her ninth birthday to charity: water, the NPO we first introduced in Chapter 3. She was hoping to raise $300 and bring clean drinking water to 15 people in Africa who had to drink dirty water that made them sick. She came up a little short, and only raised $220. She told her mom that she would try harder next year. But, tragically, Rachel was killed in a car accident one month after her birthday.

As word started to spread of this inspiring young girl who gave up her last birthday to help others, people began donating to her cause, and sharing the story with others who donated and shared, and so on. Within months, almost 32,000 people from around the world had donated to her cause. Rachel's last wish ended up raising $1.2 million, which has brought clean drinking water to nearly 40,000 people.[4]

In addition to the viral potential of sharing acts of service and compassion, another beauty of this type of digital exposure is that the person reading the inspiring story is already using a device that easily allows her to go to your business's website to learn more. She doesn't have to remember the business's name for some other time; she can begin to find out more immediately, while still most inspired by what she saw.

Although we could certainly get a funny post or video to go viral as well, humor only creates a topical level of interest. We laugh and think, "I like them," but the bond doesn't go much deeper than that. People are not likely to develop high levels of trust and loyalty with a company just because it made them laugh. This is why a lot of companies notice that their viral "funny" campaigns often don't result in any significant increases in sales.

Compassion touches something deep in us. Research shows that we experience the same level of enjoyment when we witness a compassionate act as we would if we had actually performed the compassionate act ourselves. And the enjoyment we feel is the highest level of happiness and well-being that we can experience. Matthieu Ricard, who has been found by researchers using fMRI brain scans to be by far the happiest person ever measured by science,[5] was asked how he created such a joyful state of mind at the time he was measured. His reply was, "I was meditating on boundless compassion for all beings."

Research has also shown that the joy that we receive from compassion and service lasts significantly longer than the joy that occurs as a result of humor or entertainment. When we're inspired by an act of compassion, we don't just share something once or twice and forget about it. We remember it and can share it for years. So when a current or potential customer is inspired by an organization's acts of compassion, they not only think, "I like them" (which is all we get with humor), but they also think things like, "They make me feel good. They inspire me. I trust them.

I would do business with them. I want to tell others about them."
And people often continue to tell others about that organization
for years.

We can facilitate these effects of social media by sharing our
efforts to serve the community with blog or microblog (platforms
like Facebook and Twitter) posts that include high-quality photos
or videos that catch people's eye. Those of us who were raised
to give only in private, and not make a show of it, might find
the idea of sharing our acts of compassion via social media to
be a little uncomfortable. (I did at first.) However, if we're truly
interested in doing the most good, we might want to reconsider
this view.

Sharing our good works not only helps our organization,
which ensures that we can continue to have the resources to
serve, but it also inspires other organizations to do the same. The
increased ROI we experience from the marketing efforts that
serve our communities will compel other organizations to copy
us. By inspiring other organizations to serve their communities
more, we can multiply our efforts many times over. Even if their
motives are purely transactional, the communities will benefit
nonetheless.

This is a point that Bert Jacobs made so well when he shared
the story of Life is good. He, too, was raised to give in private. But
he has since changed his view, citing the logic above. He has also
realized that for-profit companies almost always attract and retain
more talented people than do NPOs, and they typically have
access to much greater resources. So Bert stressed the idea that
for-profit companies can make a much bigger impact on society
than NPOs can alone. He also made a good business case for why
companies would want to do this.

Since the day Bert and John decided to invest in helping people instead of in traditional advertising, they have never looked back. They have yet to spend a dime on traditional advertising. Their festival has grown every year to become a huge event. In 2012, Life is good had some of the biggest names in music playing at their festival—including the Dave Matthews Band—and they raised approximately $1 million for charitable causes working to help children in need.

Bert showed a historical graph of the growth curve for Life is good. It looked a lot like a hockey stick. For years it was essentially flat. Since the day Bert and John started investing in helping people as their main marketing strategy, the curve has been almost vertical.

* * *

Most of us likely remember the 2013 Boston Marathon for the horrific bombing that took place at the finish line. As Boston natives, Bert and John Jacobs were likely as saddened by this event as anyone. But in addition to teaching us about the power of making serving others our chief marketing strategy, Life is good reminds us that focusing on the positive elements of life is much more skillful than focusing on the negative.

One shining example of a positive gem that came out of the 2013 Boston Marathon was a recent college graduate who had flown in from San Francisco to be part of the Mass General Hospital team. Although she didn't finish the full marathon, she did finish the first half in just over 2 hours and 20 minutes, which is a great feat in and of itself. It requires a very high level of athleticism to finish a half marathon in that amount of time.

But what makes the feat awe inspiring is that her name is Lindsey Beggan. And, as of this writing, she has been cancer free for 14 years.

Wouldn't it be nice if your organization had a story like that to share? You could—if you make helping others the central element of your marketing strategy.

Part 3
Making the Shift: Becoming the Ultimate Leader

7 Making Serving a Habit

John Spence is a bulky, barrel-chested man. He looks like he was born to play rugby, which he did for much of his life, and he has several gnarly fingers that were once badly broken to show for it. He also has an infectious smile and what seems to be a never-ending supply of energy.

In 1992, John was 26 years old and working as a public relations manager for a division of the Rockefeller Foundation called The Billfish Foundation. Although he had graduated from the University of Florida only three years earlier, John quickly made a name for himself there. The ideas he offered up during the board meetings he attended were implemented a disproportionate amount of the time, and at the age of only 26, John was named CEO of the foundation. He began overseeing projects in 20 countries and reporting directly to the Chairman of the Board, Winthrop P. Rockefeller III.

John did very well. Three years later, *Inc.* magazine's Zinc Online recognized him as one of America's up and coming young business leaders. After leaving the Billfish Foundation, he went on to work as an interim CEO for companies that were failing and he helped turn several of them around. He then began working as a consultant, developing executives into more effective leaders.

John has twice been named one of the Top 100 Business Thought Leaders in America by Trust Across America, and he has appeared on their global list of the Top 100 Thought Leaders in the area of "Trustworthy Business Behavior." He has presented workshops, speeches, and executive coaching to more than 300 organizations worldwide including Microsoft, GE, Merrill Lynch, AT&T, government offices, and numerous NPOs. He is the author of *Awesomely Simple*[1] and has been a guest lecturer at over 90 colleges and universities across the United States.

It is quite safe to say that John Spence is an "expert" in his field with a tremendous amount of knowledge to share. He is affectionately referred to as the "Human Cliffs Notes" by many of his clients. In addition to his real-world experience, for the past 19 years John has read an average of 100 business-related books each year and listened to another 30 to 50 audio books. What is most interesting about John Spence, though, is that he continues this level of reading and studying to this day. He hasn't stopped learning and has no plans to do so anytime soon.

Part Three of this book is about making the shift to becoming what I call the *ultimate leader*—the type of leader who easily achieves the business outcomes we discussed in Part Two. This is someone who is always leading by example—whether or not she has a title—by being an awesome human being. She knows that to lead others is to *serve others*, so everything she does is motivated by the aspiration to serve, including taking care of herself to ensure that she is happy and healthy, so she is best able to serve the people around her.

Another one of the ultimate leader's key traits is her commitment to continuously growing both personally and professionally, motivated by the aspiration to serve others. Because continuously learning is perhaps the easiest step we can take toward continuously growing, we'll start there.

John Spence is a great living example of this trait. He is someone who is clearly committed to lifelong learning. But what's most interesting about John's insatiable appetite for knowledge is that his motivation for learning is to have more to offer other people. He is motivated by the aspiration to serve others.

John is relentless in his efforts to serve. He gives away so much great knowledge to his clients that less savvy consultants wonder how he stays in business. He spends a lot of his time sitting down to meet with local leaders and business owners, helping them to improve their organizations. I'm fortunate to count myself amongst the people with whom he has shared a tremendous amount of knowledge, which has been very helpful in terms of growing my business.

An Easy Way to Jump in to the Top 1 Percent

How many books related to personal or professional development would you guess the average college graduate reads each year once he finishes school? Five? Two? I was as surprised as you'll likely be when I learned the answer. According to John Spence, the average college graduate reads *one* personal or professional development every two years, or one-half of a book per year.

Although learning this may be cause for alarm, it should also highlight an opportunity. If we read more books on personal or professional development, we will really stand apart from those around us. According to John, reading just one book per month would put us in the top 1 percent of professionals in the country. This simple practice of reading business books and sharing the ideas he learned is essentially what got John promoted to CEO at the age of 26.

There are two primary benefits to reading books more frequently. First, the more we learn, the more we have to offer the people around us. When people bring issues to us that they're struggling with, we are more likely to either be able to share ideas that can be helpful or point people to resources to that can help them.

Second, reading books on personal and professional development can help us to become more successful individuals and better leaders. There are so many elements that go into being the best we can be, so that we in turn are best able to serve others. Diet, exercise, emotional health, time management, organization, communication, physical health, emotional health, strategic planning, execution of strategies and tactics, and so forth all play a role in how effective we are as leaders. We don't have to reinvent the proverbial wheel with any of these topics. If we're struggling with one of the many elements of being an effective leader, there is certainly someone who is an expert in the field who has written a book that can help us.

Most of us know that we should be reading frequently to augment our personal growth. The hardest part for many is finding the time to fit reading in. I recommend actually carving out time each day to get in at least 30 minutes of reading. If you do that, you should easily be able to get in one book per month and move yourself into the top 1 percent for personal development.

Action Is Most Important

We've all heard the saying "Knowledge is power," but is that necessarily true? Does having knowledge about something inherently result in positive effects? Clearly, knowledge alone is not enough. In order for knowledge to be of any use, we need to be able to apply it to either help others, or help us to grow so that we can in turn be of greater service to those around us.

While reading the rest of this book—essentially, a how-to manual for making the shift to becoming the ultimate leader—take a moment to pause after reading about an idea or tool that you believe can help you to make that shift and ask, "How can I begin applying this to my life today?" Reading more books on personal and professional development is the easiest to implement of all the ideas and tools we'll discuss.

Most thought leaders include a list of their favorite books on their blog or website. If you visit the sites of a couple of people you'd like to learn from, you can begin by immediately ordering the first book that grabs your attention. (I've included a list of both my favorite thought leaders and my favorite books on my site.) If you commit to spending about 30 minutes per day reading at some point, you'll easily be able to read most books in less than a month. If you can only squeeze in 15 minutes, then start with 15 minutes. Start with whatever amount of time you think you can realistically accomplish. If you can stick with it, you'll eventually form a good habit that will serve you and others for the rest of your life.

The Habit of Serving Others

In the same way that we can make a habit of reading, or any other activity, we can also gradually make serving others a "habit" of sorts. This approach can become the motivation for everything we do—part of our natural, automatic response to those around us. We'll discuss many ways to make this shift, starting with the simple practice of employing the skillful use of two questions. These two questions can help us form new, very powerful mental habits that benefit both ourselves and those around us.

The first question is the one I mentioned in Chapter 2: "How will this—whatever I'm doing in this moment—help me to serve others?" This question can become a filter for our decisions. Before we do something, or consume something, we can simply ask, "How will this help me to serve others?" Simply asking this question makes us more conscious of whether these are things we actually *need* to be happy and healthy and best able to serve others, or if they are just things we *want*. As we concentrate on only doing what we need, we become more effective as leaders—and happier as well.

We can also use this question when we encounter unpleasant situations or significant challenges in life. When faced with difficulties or obstacles, you can simply ask, "How will this help me to serve others?" This can provide clarity and perspective and help you see other possibilities or solutions. When you are experiencing something unpleasant or challenging, immediately start thinking about what you are meant to learn from the situation, and consider how what you're learning can help you to serve others.

The second question is, "What can I do to better serve those around me?" Whether or not you have an official title or position of authority, continuously asking this question can transform your perspectives, your choices, and your actions. Instead of thinking, "What can I get out of my team?" or "How can I leverage my employees to advance *my* career?" you can form a new mental habit when you start asking, "What can I *give* the people on my team?" Think about how you can help the members of your team to be happier both at home and at work, and help them grow personally and professionally.

Of course, as leaders, we need to set very clear expectations and let those we lead know that they will be held accountable to those expectations. However, we don't need to focus our energy there. Once expectations are set, we should focus energy on serving members of our team. And, as we discussed in Part Two, this shift is a much more effective way to "get more out of people" and "advance our careers." When we concentrate on serving others, we don't need to "motivate" them to meet expectations. They'll most likely exceed those expectations—and not because they have to, but because they want to.

One of the easiest ways to serve is to help your team continuously develop—both personally and professionally. Even if you currently have nothing in the budget to spend on training, there are some low-cost approaches to investing in your team. You could personally teach a class every week on skills that you've developed. This serves the dual purpose of helping you to become a better presenter, while sending the message to your team that you truly care about them. Making that kind of commitment tells employees that you are willing to spend an hour of your salary and theirs just to help them grow.

Another low-cost option is to create a library of personal and professional development books at the office, which can start with books you've read as a result of your new habit. You could even start a book club. Team members can all read a different book a month and spend a couple of hours discussing the topics as a team. Your team will benefit from getting an overview of several books per month, and this practice will help them to develop critical thinking and presentation skills.

If you can afford it, you should establish a budget for bringing in outside trainers as well. Spending money on such efforts sends a very powerful message, especially when the topic is one that employees can apply to improve both their professional and personal lives. It lets them know, "We care about you so much that we're willing to invest a good deal of money in your growth."

As Jeffery Krames pointed out in his book *What the Best CEOs Know,*[2] this was the key principle practiced by legendary General Electric (GE) CEO Jack Welch. Although he was known for being quite ruthless in his management style, Jack's main focus during the 20 years he spent at GE was transforming the company into a learning organization. During his tenure, GE invested a tremendous amount of money in developing employees. Spending a few years at GE during this time was essentially like being paid to get an MBA. It is very easy to attract top talent when people know that working for you can dramatically increase their future success.

The ultimate leader takes this idea of developing the people on her team even further. She aims to develop people to the point where they could easily do her job. She knows something that very few up-and-coming leaders know: One of the best forms of evidence of great leadership is successfully developing future leaders. She's not worried that she might lose her job because she has helped someone become as capable as—or more capable than—her. She knows that when her seniors see that she has developed people who can do her job, they'll know that she's 100 percent devoted to the organization's long-term success—and clearly ready for more responsibility.

There is a variety of tactics you can employ to better serve the people around you and help them grow. But a great first step for making the shift from thinking, "What can I get out of people?" to "What can I give?" is committing at least 10 minutes per day to asking: "How can I *better serve* the people around me?" and contemplating possible answers. In the following chapters you'll find many ways to better serve the people on your team. Part of this time of reflection could include questions specific to how you could better apply the ideas from those chapters that most resonate with you. You can gradually work up to 15 to 20 minutes or more, but 10 is a good start. Again, if it's realistic, it's more likely to become a habit.

Make this the absolute first thing you do when starting your work day. Skip the e-mails. Forget about the to-do lists. Start with thinking about how you can better serve the people on your team. This will set the tone for the morning and inform your decisions and interactions with others in ways that could transform both your organization and your life.

The Little Things Matter

I tend to think big. One of the most important insights that has come out of my monastic training is that the little things we do moment to moment are just as important, if not more so, than our big accomplishments. We can do big things in life, but if we don't treat people right along the way, it's all for naught. So although I still set big goals, I no longer let those goals get in the way of doing the little things that make life truly rich, like treating people with kindness and compassion, and doing what I can to leave people a little better off than I found them.

Every time we interact with another person, we have the opportunity to do something that is either neutral or negative—or add value to his life. I've noticed that it doesn't take much to lift a person up. Sometimes just a smile or a small act of kindness or compassion does the trick, like taking a moment to listen to someone who is hurting and letting him know that it's perfectly okay for him to be sad in our presence—we'll just be with him without judgment. Making an effort to leave each person at least a little better off than we found him is one of the most powerful things we can do, whether we have a title or not, to make the shift toward becoming the ultimate leader.

When we consistently offer our smile and treat others with kindness and compassion, we make it part of our routine to show people we care about them. And when people feel truly cared for, they are much more likely to follow us. As we discussed in Chapter 2, this is the most effective tool there is for building influence with others.

One way to do this is to ask the following question, silently in your mind, whenever you begin interacting with another person: "What can I do to help this person?" You don't need to have an answer right away; you just need to ask the question. A way to help her may present itself while you interact, afterward, or maybe not at all. What's most important is that you set the intention for the interaction as one of service. People will pick up on this unconscious signal that you care about them. They'll likely feel good when they're around you, even though they might not be sure why. You definitely don't need a title to attract people to you when they feel good in your presence. This is the essence of truly great leadership.

What a Teenager Dying of Cancer Taught Me about Leadership

One of my favorite examples of how powerful doing the little things can be comes from the work I've done with Kids Kicking Cancer. As inspired as I often am by the heroes I meet through this work, I never thought that I would learn incredible lessons about leadership from a patient on a pediatric cancer unit. But that's exactly what happened in early 2013 while I was still instructing group classes for our Gainesville program.

I had the pleasure of meeting a teenager named Daniel. It didn't take long to realize that he is one of the kindest, most polite, and most positive people I have ever met. He has also lived an incredibly challenging life. Years ago, he was diagnosed with cancer. He had surgery, went through the hell of chemo and radiation therapies, and left the hospital free of cancer thinking that he would live the rest of his life without having to worry about it.

However, within a couple of years, Daniel's cancer came back. He went through the hell again, and again left the hospital thinking he was finally done with being sick.

This time, though, when the cancer came back, it was every-where. He was told that there was nothing that could be done to treat it and that he would probably only live a few more months. I spent time with him minutes after he had received this news. It was obvious that he had cried.

Daniel reminded me that it's okay for leaders to cry.

He told me that he hadn't started to cry until he saw his mother crying. Apparently, being told you're going to die is not that bad. What really hurts, he said, is seeing those you love deal with the fact that they're going to lose you soon.

Despite this news, Daniel still came to the class I led that day. In fact, he was the first to arrive and the last to leave. He was incredibly positive during the class and was a great role model for the younger students.

Daniel reminded me that great leaders continue to lead by example, even when things are really, really tough.

A few days later, I was spending time with Daniel in his room. He had just eaten a large meal, and he was playing a video game and chatting with me in between levels. After a few moments, the woman who delivers the hospital meals came in. She placed the food on the table on wheels, and slid the table to the bed so that it fit snugly against Daniel's chest.

This forced Daniel to pause his game. But, he looked at the woman with a smile, and thanked her sincerely. The woman smiled as she left. The moment the door closed, he pushed the table away from the bed, having no interest in the food, and went back to playing his game.

Although it was barely noticeable, that was a very powerful moment for me. I consider myself a fairly kind and patient person, but I'm quite certain that if I were Daniel I would have politely told the woman that I wasn't hungry and that she could leave the food over on the table away from the bed.

But Daniel didn't do that. After receiving the worst news you could ever receive only a few days earlier, he was so sensitive to the woman's feelings that he allowed her to do her job and thanked her for it—despite the fact that she had interrupted his game and he had no interest in the food. He did it because, as he later told me, he knew that it would make her feel good.

He knew what all great leaders know—that there's nothing more important in leadership and in life than doing what we can to make the people around us happy.

A few days later, I spoke with a friend of mine who is a director at a Fortune 100 company. She told me about a VP who used different variations of the f-word nearly 20 times during the meeting he led that afternoon. At one point, he told the people at the meeting that he doesn't give a "f—" about them. He later said to not take it personally because he wears his emotions on his sleeve, and that when he's having a bad day people will know he's having a bad day.

People left that meeting feeling completely demoralized, with no desire to follow him anywhere. I wouldn't be surprised if some of them actually began plotting ways to do less than before, and maybe even help him get fired so that they won't have to deal with him anymore.

When I heard this, I thought of Daniel, and I cried. I thought, "That VP has no idea what a bad day is."

I wished Daniel could lead those people. Daniel has the emotional intelligence and strength of character to go through years of hell that will likely culminate in watching his mother watch him die and, burdened with this knowledge, still be able to treat a woman who delivers food in the hospital who had just disrupted him as though she is the most important person in the world.

What could the people at that Fortune 100 company achieve if they had a leader who was more like Daniel?

Greatness.

8 Grow by Empowering Others

Chris Hurn is the co-founder and CEO of Mercantile Capital Corporation in Orlando, Florida. In the spring of 2012, he had to travel to California for business and was unable to attend a vacation with his wife and two children. His family stayed at the Ritz-Carlton during their beach getaway. When they got home, they noticed that they couldn't find their son's stuffed giraffe, Joshie. The boy was very attached to the toy and became upset when he realized that he might not be able to sleep with his best buddy that night.

Chris told his son (hoping it was true) that "Joshie is fine" and that "He's just taking an extra-long vacation at the resort." His son believed him, and was eventually able to fall asleep without it.

A little later that night, a representative from the Ritz-Carlton called to tell Chris and his wife that they found Joshie in the laundry and that he had been given to the hotel's Loss Prevention Team. Chris shared the story he had told his son with the staff and asked if they would be so kind as to get a picture of Joshie relaxing by the pool, which would make the story come true for his son. The team happily complied.

A couple days later, Chris received a package from the hotel. Inside was Joshie, along with a frisbee, football, and a couple of other toys branded with the Ritz-Carlton logo. The package also included a binder that detailed everything Joshie did during his extended stay at the hotel. There were photos of Joshie wearing shades by the pool, making friends, getting a massage at the spa, and even driving a golf cart on the beach. The package also included a Ritz-Carlton ID badge made for Joshie, listing him as an honorary member of the Loss Prevention Team, as well as a photo of him working a shift, monitoring the security monitors.[1]

This example of world-class customer service didn't cost the Ritz-Carlton much. It simply required a lot of thoughtfulness on the part of the staff. But it's the perfect example of the lengths to which Ritz-Carlton employees go to wow a guest.

Sometimes, though, the things they do to create a "wow" moment for guests require more of a financial investment, such as what occurred at their hotel in Bali.

Two guests there had a boy with serious food allergies. Because of the allergies, the family always made it a point to bring their own supply of specialized eggs and milk when they went on vacation. However, the food was rendered useless en route to Bali. The manager on duty couldn't find any of the special foods the boy needed in the country; however, his executive chef stated that he knew of a store in Singapore that *did* sell them. They contacted the chef's mother-in-law, who lived in Singapore, and paid for her to purchase the items and then fly to Bali, over two hours away, to deliver them.

Employees at the Ritz-Carlton don't have to ask permission to do these types of things. They have been empowered by their leaders to make decisions like this on their own and on the spot. For many of us, the thought of giving employees the degree of autonomy mentioned here, or in the stories in Chapter 5, might evoke the emotion of fear. But if we want to be highly effective leaders, we absolutely must get comfortable with the idea of empowering team members to the greatest extent possible.

Empowered People Equal Better Results

The following quote—attributed to Lao-Tzu, considered by many to be the wisest man in the history of China—summarizes a true leader's achievement: "When the best leader's work is done the people say, 'We did it ourselves!'" There are many, many reasons, in addition to realizing the benefits of offering world-class service, why empowering people results in better outcomes.

First, empowering team members can dramatically improve our organization's capacity for innovation. As Tim Ferris pointed out in his bestselling book *The 4-Hour Workweek*,[2] "It's amazing how someone's IQ seems to double as soon as you give them responsibility and indicate that you trust them." Tim outsources almost all of his daily, routine tasks to independent contractors like virtual assistants. He tells them that they have the authority to spend up to $100, without asking permission, to make sure that any one customer is happy. When we find ways like this to empower people, we significantly reduce bureaucracy, which frees team members up to be more innovative.

We might not be able to prove that someone's IQ actually doubles when we empower them, but in his bestselling book *Drive*,[3] Daniel Pink draws on 40 years of research showing how much more effective providing autonomy is as a motivator than is money. He points out how this is especially true for any work that requires creativity and other forms of higher-level thinking, which is almost all work in the business world. A great real-world example of this principle in action is Google's flextime.

Google employees are allowed and strongly encouraged to spend up to 20 percent of their time on campus working on any project they want to. In other words, they can spend a full day out of each work week on pet projects that excite them. The only requirement is that they need to report on what they're working on from time to time. Google reports that as much as 50 percent of the company's innovations are the result of projects that employees have conceived and developed during flextime.

Second, empowered people like coming to work more—and who wouldn't want the members on their team to actually look forward to coming to work? Besides being the right thing to do, creating an enjoyable team culture results in greater productivity, more innovation, and a significant impact on a company's ability to attract and retain top talent.

Empowering the people on a team can also save a tremendous amount of time. When people know that we trust them and even expect them to make decisions without our input, we can eliminate having to think about and answer questions that they're fully qualified to answer on their own. We are freed up to focus our energy on higher-level and more strategic aspects of our work, and on serving the members of our team. This is vitally important for any leader, but especially for start-up entrepreneurs. One of the easiest ways to speed up the growth of a newer organization is to delegate as much responsibility as possible to others so that we can work on our business and our culture instead of being constantly caught up in the day-to-day operations.

Empowering Others Helps Us Become the Ultimate Leaders

It's very natural to want to have control over every action team members take. This is especially true when we're first promoted to a leadership position and when we're really good at what we do, which is why most people get promoted. Unfortunately, this is not a good reason to get promoted in and of itself. Although competency is certainly important because people are unlikely to follow an incompetent leader, it's a very poor predictor of how *effective* a person will be as a leader. In fact, when we work with leaders who are undergoing a Perth Leadership Institute training course, we spend a good deal of time demonstrating how a person's greatest strength will actually become a huge liability when he reaches the level of general management.

Developing the ability to give up control and the feeling that we need to do everything ourselves is an absolutely essential element of our basic leadership development. Making an effort to empower people is also a great tool for helping make the shift to becoming the ultimate leader. Taking little steps every day to empower others helps us to gradually become less focused on ourselves and more focused on serving others.

So let's look at some ideas and tools for helping us to become increasingly comfortable with extending high levels of trust to members of our team and truly empowering them, so that we can gradually make that a new mental habit.

The Power of Listening

According to Dr. Stephen Covey, the bestselling author of *The 7 Habits of Highly Effective People*,[4] seeking to understand others before we seek to be understood is the single most important interpersonal skill we can develop. It's also an essential element of being a good leader. Although not very easy, one of the simplest things we can do to empower team members is to do more listening and less talking.

In early 2013, I had a lunch meeting with Dr. Ted Prince of the Perth Leadership Institute, the man I first introduced you to in Chapter 3. The topic of listening came up during our lunch. It reminded Dr. Prince of three essential rules for communicating better during a meeting, which he had learned over his 20-year career as a CEO and had recently taught to some executives he was now coaching:

1. **Speak last.** As leaders, we often think that *we're* supposed to be the one with all the ideas. But effective leaders know how necessary it is to surround ourselves with people that are smarter than us and find ways to get them sharing ideas as frequently as possible. Speaking last is a great way to make sure this happens. When we speak first, we can create unconscious boxes from which people might not feel safe deviating. By making the effort to get team members talking before we share any of our own thoughts, we ensure that we have the best chance of getting fresh, new ideas that we might have never heard if we shared our ideas first.

2. **Speak less than 10 percent of the time.** When we do speak, it should be at most 10 percent of the time, and primarily to ask questions. We already know what we think about the topic; the only way we'll discover solutions that are potentially better than the ones we have is to get others talking as much as possible. In this way, they are likely to either create a solution or provide some new way of looking at an issue that allows us

to arrive at a solution that we never would have seen had we tried to do it all on our own.

3. **Don't offer opinions.** Our goal is to create an environment in which people feel safe to share whatever ideas they have. The moment we start offering opinions about the topic in general—or, worse, an idea someone has shared—we cause people to worry about sharing ideas and decrease the likelihood that we will get truly innovative solutions.

Setting Boundaries

There is a legitimate concern about giving team members "free rein" to do whatever is needed to wow customers. We might worry that they'll spend more than is appropriate, or make some other kind of rash decision. Although I think it's natural to have thoughts like this, there is really no need to worry about it because when we care for and trust people, they almost always do the right thing.

That being said, we can also reduce the risk of some anomaly to the general rule of people doing the right thing by setting boundaries that give members of our team some structure for how they can go about wowing a customer. This is as simple as placing a limit on how much a team member can spend on any single customer, which can vary depending on the margins of our products or services.

As previously mentioned, Tim Ferris sets a limit of $100. The Ritz-Carlton sets a limit of $2,000. The logic is exactly the same in either case: Leaders at the Ritz-Carlton are saying to team members, "We trust you do the right thing to make sure that our customers are 100 percent satisfied with their experience with us.

You can be as creative as you like to make that happen, and spend as much as $2,000 per customer to make that happen." In most cases, the employees spend almost nothing to come up with creative ways to wow a customer, as was the case with Chris Hurn and his son's Joshie. But, when it's necessary—as with the family staying at the Bali hotel—employees have the freedom to make some big decisions without getting approval.

Core Values Make Decisions Easy

Another way to create a bit of structure for giving people freedom to decide on their own is to apply the power of core values. In order to run a highly successful organization, we need to have absolute clarity on our core values and communicate those core values well and as often as possible. Everyone in an organization should be able to easily recite them from memory and understand exactly what they mean.

One benefit to having this kind of clarity is that it facilitates the hiring process. Organizations that maintain great cultures even as they grow tend to hire for culture fit and train for skills. As long as candidates meet the minimum skill requirements for a position, managers base their hiring decisions on who is the best fit for the culture. If a candidate's core values are significantly different from the organization's values, the person is clearly not a good fit for the culture.

Another benefit is that it makes decision making very easy for people. Well-designed core values should act as filters for decisions. When faced with a decision, people should be able to run the options through each of the core values, starting with the first. If an option would violate one of the core values, it can immediately be eliminated as a possible course of action. For instance, if one of our core values is *long-term success*, when a member of our team has to decide whether to do something that will result in short-term gain, but could result in negative long-term consequences, she will know that the course of action being considered is not even an option.

Core values allow us to give team members even more autonomy. If our core values are well thought out, we should be able to say to the people we lead, "I hired you because I have great confidence that you will make good decisions. So, although you are welcome to seek my input on any decision, these are the only things that you need my approval on (there may be a several examples where you will want to have the final say). With everything else, provided that what you do is in line with our core values, it's your call. I trust you to do the right thing. Don't be afraid to make a mistake. As long as it doesn't violate our core values, making mistakes will just help you learn and grow."

When we apply core values in this way, it is much easier for us to make new mental habits that will empower people and help us move in the direction of becoming the ultimate leaders. One such mental habit is refraining from telling people how to do things. We will feel a lot more comfortable about simply giving team members clear, binary goals without telling them how to achieve the goal. (A binary goal removes ambiguity; it is either achieved or not achieved.) When we make a habit out of leaving the "how" up to the people we lead, we will notice several benefits: It saves time, it helps people grow, and we'll find that team members often come up with better ways of doing things than we would have.

Inclusive Decisions versus Commands

Another simple way to empower the people on our team is to get them involved in decisions *we* make. Instead of taking a command approach in which we make most or all decisions without getting the input of other people, we include others on as many decisions as possible. There are many benefits to shifting from the command approach to an approach that gets people more involved in the decision-making process.

First, the inclusive approach often actually helps us to make better decisions. As great as we might think we are, it's almost impossible to consider every angle to an issue. Having different perspectives on a problem is vital, and this becomes even more essential the further removed we are from an issue. Getting the input of people who are closer to the action can be extremely helpful. For example, if we run a retail store, simply asking a frontline team member what she notices about how customers respond to our checkout counter could provide invaluable insights into unconscious behaviors of the customers that we couldn't get even by directly asking the customer.

Another benefit to getting people involved in decisions is that it builds trust, and high levels of trust in an organization are very closely correlated to high levels of performance. In an organization in which trust is lacking, failure is not far away.

The inclusive approach also creates an ownership mentality. When people are involved in a decision, they feel as though they are valued members of the team and they are much more likely to consistently act in the organization's best interests.

Although it may sound counterintuitive, the inclusive approach to decisions is usually more efficient. Of course, it would be faster in the short run to simply have a command-and-control-type leader who simply barks orders at people. But it can actually result in significantly longer implementation times.

HFE CEO Joel Manby describes very clearly why this is so in his excellent book *Love Works*: "[Autocratic decision making] is almost always less effective, because others in the organization may not support the decision. As a result, team members can help 'make it fail' in their own unique ways, and they certainly won't be as energetic about the unilateral decision. A leader may decide something, but the whole organization needs to execute it.....When team members know they are trusted enough to be part of the decision-making process in advance, their support of the decision will be stronger and the implementation of that decision will be faster and more effective."[5]

Tools for Fast, Inclusive Decisions

It is certainly not an easy task to make decisions quickly while also getting people involved, but it becomes markedly easier when we have effective tools in place to facilitate the process. In *Love Works*, Joel also offers a great example of such a tool that HFE has implemented with great results. The method he describes is referred to as RACI, an acronym that outlines a four-step process:

1. **Responsible:** The first step is to clarify who is ultimately responsible for making the decision.

2. **Approve:** The second step is to clarify who needs to approve the decision to ensure that it is sound.

3. **Consult:** Before a decision becomes final, we need to consult with the people who will be affected in some way.

4. Inform: Once a decision has been reached, team members who are not directly affected should be informed of the decision and its rationale.

Although it can take a little time up front to ensure that the RACI process is followed, it is definitely time well spent. When people feel involved in the decision process and understand *how* they are involved, trust is built and maintained, and confusion and hurt feelings are reduced or eliminated. *Love Works* also features an actual diagram of how the RACI process was applied for a real-world decision at HFE.

What's the next decision you need to make that involves members of your team? Perhaps you could implement the RACI process and discover for yourself how well it works.

Holacracy

Holacracy[6] is similar to RACI, although it's a more intricate and expansive tool. It is a very powerful tool for increasing productivity employed by the staff at the David Allen Company. David Allen is the author of the mega-best-seller *Getting Things Done*, and is perhaps the most respected authority on productivity in the world. Holacracy is also used by Obvious Corporation (founded by Brian Evans of Twitter), Adscale Laboratories, and the staff of Conscious Capitalism.

Holacracy empowers members of an organization by getting them involved in the decision-making process and giving them authority. The foundation of holacracy's effectiveness, similar to the RACI method, is the clarity that's created around who should be responsible for what decisions. These roles are determined in regular governance meetings and are allowed to evolve based on real-world feedback from people.

The most striking and empowering feature of the governance clarity is that once it is determined that a person is in charge of a certain element of the business—like marketing, for instance—that person has the ultimate say on everything that has been determined to fall completely under the marketing umbrella. Although the CEO could provide input on the decision, not even she has the authority to overrule the decision of the person deemed "in charge." Imagine how empowered an employee must feel when he is told that not even the CEO can overrule decisions he makes on his area of authority.

The regular operational/tactical meetings speed up tremendously as a result of this clarification on who has authority over what. As each agenda item is raised, everyone at the meeting is asked if they have any data that would affect a decision on the next action. Then ideas for the next action are solicited. At that point, the discussion is over. The person in charge of the area being discussed makes a decision on the next action and the meeting moves on.

When an organization employs the holacracy system, every agenda item gets processed at every meeting on time, every time. The focus is on next actions, not endless analysis, so everyone leaves with a clear sense of what he or she needs to do. Metrics surface and checklists are reviewed very quickly. In short, a tremendous amount gets done, very quickly, in a way that involves the entire team via clearly identified roles.

There is also a clear process for raising what's called a *tension,* which is any gap between the current reality and how things should ideally be. Anyone in the organization can raise tensions. If the secretary notices something that isn't working in quality, he has the right to raise the tension—and that tension will be heard and addressed in the same efficient manner as any other agenda item. Not only does this empower team members by giving them a true voice; it also benefits the overall organization tremendously. Oftentimes the best ideas come from people who are looking from the outside in. Holacracy provides an efficient way to tap in to what is often an overlooked resource—the frontline people.

In June of 2013, I interviewed Brian Burt, who serves as CEO of MaestroConference,[7] an online social conferencing company that has served clients ranging from small businesses to the campaign for President Barack Obama. MaestroConference had been implementing holacracy for about two years when we spoke. Brian mentioned how several members of his team had stated, "the worst holacracy meeting I've ever been in is better than the best meeting I've ever been in anywhere else."

Brian also mentioned that the amount of time they spend in meetings has gone down significantly. At scale, having senior leaders spend less time in meetings could result in incredible cost savings. For instance, let's imagine that the average salary of 20 people in a meeting is $100,000, which is roughly $50 per hour. If we could shorten meetings from four hours per week to one hour per week, that would result in an instant annual reduction in costs of $156,000.

This cost reduction does not take into account the increases in revenues that result by improving our culture. During our interview, Brian also mentioned that only a couple of years earlier, he was getting feedback from employees that they often didn't enjoy coming to work. Brian is passionate about creating a culture that people want to be a part of, but something was missing. Apparently, that something was *empowerment*.

Within weeks of implementing holacracy, the entire culture had made a complete 180-degree turn. People reported that they felt empowered and loved coming to work at MaestroConference. Surely, I thought, there must have been other changes in how they did things. When I asked Brian if he had integrated any changes other than holacracy, he told me, "It was night and day, and instant, and only with holacracy." Empowering the people at MastroConference was enough to transform the culture.

9 Inspire Greatness

Anyone who has visited Washington, DC, in the summer can attest to the fact that it can be brutally hot and humid. I first learned about this during my officer training for the Marine Corps. Prior to arriving—and almost daily while attending officer candidates school and the six-month-long basic school in Quantico, which is just outside of DC—we were briefed on the all the precautions we should be taking to prevent heat injury. The heat alone could be enough to deter many people from attending an all-day, outdoor event on an August day in DC.

There were other, rather convincing reasons to miss out on one particular outdoor event in August—a march on the nation's capitol. One was the fact that many people would have to travel for hours to arrive, and they didn't have their own transportation. Another was that authorities of many types were warning people *not* to attend the event because they expected it to be very dangerous due to racial tensions.

It was also no easy task to invite all the people who should be there. There was no e-mail at this time, or Facebook, or website people could visit for details. The most cost-effective way to invite people was via word of mouth.

But something interesting happened on the morning of August 28, 1963. People came. Lots of them. Despite having to travel up to eight hours by bus, and despite being told that it might be unsafe, people from many ethnic groups came from many places near and far. Religious leaders from nearly every faith gathered in harmony. This diverse group, which ended up numbering roughly 250,000 people, the largest gathering in Washington, DC, to date at the time, was described as being so peaceful that it was compared by witnesses to being at a church picnic. This march on Washington has been remembered ever since as one of the most important dates in our nation's history.

How did this happen? Why, in the face of all these obstacles, did 250,000 people attend this event? Why was the event so well-orchestrated and so successful? It's simple: The people involved were deeply inspired.

The first people to learn of the event were so inspired that they told everyone they knew about it, and systems for spreading the word appeared quite organically. Those who attended were so inspired that they traveled from far and wide to get there and stand all day in the Washington, DC, summer heat. They were also so inspired by the cause that they adopted it as their own and organically agreed to follow the values that guided the efforts to bring the cause to life.

The principal source of their inspiration was a young preacher named Dr. Martin Luther King, Jr. There were, of course, numerous factors that contributed to Dr. King becoming the de facto leader of the civil rights movement in America. However, it is clear that the principal cause is the fact that Dr. King was incredibly *inspiring*. He was able touch people's hearts in a way that few others in history ever have. Fortunately for us, his gifts for inspiring others and moving them to action are traits that we can all emulate. Dr. King had inspiring character and the ability to connect people to a purpose far greater than themselves.

Start with Why

Start with Why[1] author Simon Sinek is currently one of the most sought-after speakers in the world. His TED talk[2] is, as of this writing, the second-most popular of all time, with over 15 million views via the TED platforms alone. The reason for all this is that Simon made a very interesting discovery that can have a tremendous impact on the success of any organization.

Simon discovered that the most inspiring leaders in history—those who led businesses, governments, or social movements—all had something in common: They were all very clear about *why* they do what they do, which involves some version of serving a purpose greater than themselves. They were also very effective at communicating this "why" to others. In fact, Simon noticed that the most inspiring leaders all communicate in the same way, which is the exact opposite of how most people communicate.

Most people talk about *what* they do or what their organization does first. Then they talk about *how* they do it. But most people never talk about their "why." Conversely, the most inspiring leaders start with "why." Then they talk about how they bring their cause to life. Then they talk about what it is that they do.

Dr. King was a perfect example of this principle in action. As Simon points out in his book, Dr. King did not go around speaking about detailed plans for how to change civil rights in America. Dr. King spoke about his cause, about his beliefs. He spoke about his vision of a world where all people are treated equally. His most famous speech, given that day in Washington, DC, in 1963, has been referred to ever since as "I Have a Dream."

Simon summarized his idea with an image called the *Golden Circle*. The innermost circle is "why," surrounded by a ring for "how," surrounded by a ring for "what." He first began talking about the Golden Circle based simply on the anecdotal evidence he found in his own story of turning his life around and the stories of so many great leaders that applied this principle. He found one example after another of highly successful leaders who started with "why" and of leaders who failed when they didn't. As Simon continued to speak about the Golden Circle, he later learned that the effects of starting with "why" and even the Golden Circle itself, are actually based on the brain's biology.

The brain can be divided into three basic parts, which correspond to the three sections of the Golden Circle: the limbic system (why), the middle brain (how), and the most complex part of the brain, the neocortex (what). Although the neocortex allows us to perform all the high-level cognition that separates us from other animals, that is *not* the portion of the brain that makes decisions. The portion of the brain that is responsible for ultimately making decisions is the emotional part of the brain: the limbic system.

This part of the brain can't be won over with words because it has no capacity for language. This part of the brain can only be won over when we "feel" good about making a decision. If we want someone to take action on the ideas we share, it's not enough to provide convincing arguments; we need to touch their hearts. That is, we need to inspire them.

The Gift of Inspiration

The most basic definition of being a leader is being a person who other people willingly follow. As shown by Dr. King's example, one of the most powerful ways we can compel people to follow us is to inspire them by connecting their work to a purpose far bigger than themselves. But, there are also some very specific leadership benefits to starting with "why."

First of all, this approach is very, *very* good for business. In 1989, when Bill George joined Medtronic,[3] the world's fourth-largest medical device company, as the CEO, shareholders were putting pressure on the board to focus on short-term financial objectives. The company was then valued at $1.1 billion. Bill asked a board member what he would do if an offer was made to buy the company for $2 billion, and the board member said that he would sell the company. At that moment, Bill made a vow to make Medtronic such a mission-driven, valuable company that no one would allow it to be taken over by corporate raiders.

As CEO, Bill George focused on starting with "why." The company's mission, "to alleviate pain, restore health, and extend life," was communicated clearly and very frequently. Soon enough, you could see the vision and mission everywhere at Medtronic. It was in every building, hanging on the walls, and on cards carried by every employee. Next to the mission and vision were photos of the people whose lives were changed for the better because they had Medtronic medical devices implanted in their bodies. The employees are deeply inspired by the vision and mission and it guides their daily work.

Bill George knows that the secret to creating long-term value for all the stakeholders in an organization is to ensure that people aren't merely focusing on short-term financial objectives. They need to be inspired. As he wrote in his excellent book, *Authentic Leadership*:[4] "The authentic way to increase shareholder value is with a mission that inspires employees to create innovative products and provide superior service to customers. Product innovations and superior service translate into increased market share and expanded market opportunities, creating growth in revenues and the ability to sustain price levels. This is the basis for sustained competitive advantage, increased levels of profitability, and higher profit margins. Consistent profit growth forms the basis for sustained increases in shareholder value."

Although there are many examples of companies that have proved the power and truth of this simple model, Medtronic itself is an excellent one. As Bill writes, "This is precisely the approach we used at Medtronic that led to a 150 times increase in shareholder value over the last 18 years."

Clearly, inspiring people is a gift to the organization because it results in superior, long-term performance. But inspiration is also a gift we can give to people—and it's a wonderful way to serve them.

There are countless studies indicating that the vast majority of people do not enjoy their work and that employee engagement levels are disturbingly low. But we don't need a study to tell us how true this is. I'm reminded that it's true on an almost daily basis based on how people respond to my greeting.

To me, every day that I am alive and breathing is a good day. Because I'm aware of this, I usually greet people with "Happy Tuesday!" or "Happy Thursday!" and so on. Almost every time, the response is some variation of, "Yeah, only ___ more days till Friday!" As a general rule, people are very fixated on the happiness that they think will come to them on the weekend. One of the most successful restaurant chains in the world is called TGI Friday's and their slogan is, "In here, it's always Friday."

Although to some degree I think that this "Happy Friday!" mentality is just a conditioned response, that conditioning is founded on the truth. Most people can't wait for the weekends because they don't enjoy their daily work. It makes me sad every time I hear it and, when I have time, I usually ask people in a kind, curious way, "What will be better about the weekend?" The typical answer is some variation of "I won't be at work."

As leaders, we can change that. If we can get very clear on how our organization is serving the greater good and clearly and frequently help people see how they are contributing to that cause, we can offer people an incredible gift. We can help them enjoy the vast majority of their lives, which is the time they spend at work.

This is something that Charlie Kim at Next Jump realized over the past few years. And because he is devoted to serving people, he immediately took action. I discussed in Chapter 3 how turnover at Next Jump is around 1 percent, compared to the industry average of 22 percent. But that wasn't the case just a few years ago. When NxJumpers received phone calls offering them two or three times what they made at Next Jump, they were more likely to leave. So Charlie started working with Simon Sinek on how to better communicate his "why," which, as it turns out, is very inspiring.

Charlie's father has always dreamed of ending world hunger. And he's smart enough to actually do it. Dr. Kim is the most famous corn scientist in the world—referred to in the Encyclopedia Britannica as the "Father of Corn"—and he has been nominated for the Nobel Prize three times. He never won because he is absolutely terrible at presenting his ideas, whether verbally or in writing. When Charlie was growing up in Nigeria, where his father was working on a major project, he noticed that people only offered to help his dad if they could get something out of it. They would say things like, "I'll help you present your ideas and win the Nobel Prize if you give me 40 percent of your patent rights." Charlie never heard anyone say, "I want to help you simply because you are a good man who is working to help a lot of people."

As Charlie's business started to grow, he realized that he could help change that. If he could run a highly successful business with a culture devoted to helping others, people would want to copy *that*. And if enough organizations employed such a business model, it would have a significant impact on our society.

With Simon's help, Charlie figured out how to communicate clearly and concisely why Next Jump exists: to do the little things that allow others to do the great things they are meant to do. Next Jump is using the business as a vehicle for making the world a better place.

These days, everyone at Next Jump is really clear on why they come to work. They don't come just to write code, or make sales, or crunch numbers. They come to work inspired because they are part of a team that is changing the world—and not even offers of triple their salary can pull them away.

Values That Inspire and Guide the Way

Once the "why" is clear and we have methods in place for consistently connecting the work people do to that "why," we can further inspire people with virtuous core values. We discussed in Chapter 8 how these core values can empower people. The reason well-constructed core values are so empowering is that they serve as a guide for how we bring our cause to life. We can essentially tell people, "You can do whatever you think is right to help us accomplish our vision and mission, provided that it is line with our core values." This frees them up to make a lot of decisions without our input.

Core values can also be a tool for inspiring people in and of themselves. When they are highly virtuous, they instill a sense of pride in being part of such a virtuous organization. Student Maid, a company that has built a very strong culture, where people find their work fulfilling, is in an industry where this is often not the case—the commercial and residential cleaning industry. Student Maid offers a great example for others to follow with their core values. Following are five of their 10 core values, with a summary of each:[5]

> **Take Your Moral Fiber:** Our entire service is based on trust. Strong, positive relationships that are open and honest are a big part of what differentiates Student Maid from most other companies. Strong relationships allow us to accomplish much more than we would be able to otherwise.
>
> **Don't Leave Us Hangin':** We work as a team, and we realize the importance of being a reliable part of that team. We understand how our actions can affect others, so we make sure to look out for our teammates.

Own It: We're not just employees—we're truly invested in the Company. Our ideas are heard; moreover, they are taken into serious consideration, and often implemented Company-wide.

Pay It Forward: We wouldn't be where we are—individually or as a Company—without the constant support of our community. We want our employees to have community values, to be contributing members of the community around us.

Speak Now or Forever Hold Your Peace: We maintain constant and open communication with the entire Student Maid™ team. Whether we have a problem, question, comment, criticism, or praise, we know it is vital that we voice our thoughts.

Wouldn't you be inspired and proud to work for a company that boasts core values like these? The answer for almost everyone is likely, "Of course," but with a caveat. Our pride and inspiration would be strongly correlated to how well the company as a whole actually lives those values. Our core values statement can't just be a document that hangs on a wall in the CEO's office. A company must communicate its core values frequently, and make it clear that they are an absolute, nonnegotiable requirement for continuing to work with the organization. As soon as one person is allowed to violate the core values more than once, we send a message to the organization that those core values are just a bunch of meaningless words that were created because someone read about them in a book (although I'm sure the book was great).

It's even more important to ensure that we, as leaders, *live* those core values at all times. By doing so, we send the message that our core values are real and that our organization is actually a virtuous one. By consistently living our core values, we also have another way to offer people the gift of inspiration.

Character That Inspires

It's pretty easy to do the right thing when the conditions are right. It's not so easy when things get tough and doing the right thing could result in serious, negative consequences in the short term for us or for our organization. But it's how we respond to these challenging situations that defines our character.

Dr. King was faced with an almost nonstop series of such situations for years as he led the civil rights movement. He went to jail for intentionally disobeying inhumane laws that perpetuated bigotry. But he did so peacefully in a way that caused no harm to others or himself. He was threatened with physical violence daily at times, but he responded nonviolently, with kindness—and most importantly, he asked his followers to do the same.

Dr. King exemplified the epitome of character, which is the hallmark of the ultimate leader. He was committed to doing the right thing for the greater good, regardless of the personal costs to him, and to responding to each and every person, regardless of how they treated him, with unconditional kindness and compassion. His character not only inspired his followers, but his antagonists as well.

This type of character touches us very deeply. There is something universal about selflessly serving the greater good with unconditional kindness and compassion. Something inside us knows that living in this way is our highest calling, and deep down in each one of us, there is a yearning to reach our full potential as human beings and live that way, too. When we see someone who lives in this way, we are reminded of our aspiration. We are moved. We are inspired.

As James Hunter points out in *The World's Most Powerful Leadership Principle*,[6] this helps explain why two of the most influential leaders in history—Jesus and Gandhi—were able to attract such large followings and have such incredible impacts on our world. Despite having no official titles, Jesus and Gandhi both influenced billions of people's behaviors and compelled people to willingly follow them. Gandhi's leadership ended the oppressive British rule over India, liberating hundreds of millions of people. Roughly one-third of the people on this planet continue to follow Jesus, and most of the people in our world base their calendar off of His birthday. They both lived lives devoted to serving the greater good and practiced unconditional love for the people around them. They had character that inspired.

True Greatness

Although we often get caught up in our achievements in this world, we all know deep down that true greatness has nothing to do with how much money our organization makes, or how many things we have. We achieve it by reaching our full potential as human beings, which we all have the capacity to do.

The first step to moving in that direction is making a daily commitment to doing what's best for the greater good at all times, even when doing so will result in short-term negative consequences for ourselves or our organization. It starts with little things, like communicating honestly and ensuring that we are not divisive or misleading. And it requires us to have tough conversations when it's in everyone's best interest to have them.

An example of such a tough conversation is how we deal with someone who is underperforming.

If we come from the command and control mode of leadership thought, we might find that we demean a person who is underperforming. This approach only leads to continued poor performance. If, however, we've decided that we see the power in being a kind, compassionate leader, we might believe it's best to avoid having a discussion about poor performance at all. Neither of those options is best for all involved, and we are certainly not serving the people on our teams *or* the organizations we work for if we allow team members to do mediocre work.

Somewhere in the middle is an approach that serves all involved. We can start the "poor performance" conversation by expressing that "we" are not doing as well as we could. Poor performance is a failure on the part of both the leader and the team member. We want to make it clear that part of our jobs as leaders is to help the people we lead to reach their full potential, and then explore some ways, if any, that we have failed to give the person what he needs, and what we can do to improve. With this type of we-centered language, we unite as a team working to help the person reach his full potential.

When dealing with a person who continues to do mediocre work after several discussions like the one above, we could add an approach that John Spence teaches to leaders around the world, called the "Four Pieces of Paper." We ask the person to write out on four pieces of paper:

1. What they will achieve in a given period that they feel adequately makes up for the previous poor performance
2. What they need from us, as their leader, to make that happen

3. What the reward should be, within reason, if they hit the mark

4. What the consequence should be if they fail

Using this approach, you might find that an employee you thought you would have to fire suddenly turns around simply because you showed her you care about her. You'll also find that if she doesn't hit the mark, you *won't* have to fire her. She'll have written "I should leave" on the fourth piece of paper. She'll see that she picked the goal and was given all the support she needed to accomplish it. If she still doesn't achieve the goal, she'll almost always see that she is simply not in the right place and voluntarily move on.

This can actually provide us with another opportunity to serve our team members. If we feel that a person is a great fit for our culture, but perhaps is just in a position that he is not suited for, we can try to find him a position in our organization where he could add value and for which he is better suited. If that's not possible, we can help him to find a position with another organization for which he might be better suited.

By making a habit out of doing the right thing at all times, we can gradually develop character that inspires those around us every day. We might not immediately become a Gandhi or Dr. King, but we could certainly develop character that is equally inspiring in the business world, like that of the founders of Infinite Energy, Inc. (IEI),[7] Darin Cook and Rich Blaser.

Darin challenged IEI employees in one of his Letters from the CEO. He told them that when faced with a decision where doing the right thing would result in short-term loss for the company or where doing something that compromises their values, or the values of the company, would result in a large gain for the company, he expects the people in his company team to do the right thing, regardless of the size of the loss or the missed opportunity.

Darin and Rich were able to grow IEI from a startup to roughly $700 million per year in revenues by their sixteenth year of operations, which is by most standards rather rapid growth. But they built the company on a foundation of impeccable values and ethics. From the beginning, they were always committed to moving slowly enough to ensure that they do the right thing at all times, even when it could result in significant loss for the company in the short term. They live the values that they ask the people at IEI to follow.

One example of this occurred shortly after they had first entered a new market. IEI provides electricity and natural gas in deregulated markets, where the utilities focus on delivering the energy and companies like IEI are allowed to supply the energy that the utilities deliver to the consumer. At that time in New Jersey, IEI's only product was a one-year fixed rate. The only reason consumers would want a fixed rate was to lock in a price in the summer, when prices are historically low, to prevent the risk of paying very high prices in the winter. Fixed rates are something that the utilities did not offer as a product.

But this particular year, the utilities in New Jersey decided that they were going to lock their rates as well, ensuring that rates would not change during the winter. This was not a product offering. It was just an internal decision for that year. Thus, suppliers like IEI were informed of the rate lock, but the consumers were not.

Darin and Rich had to make a decision. They could continue to sell their fixed rates that summer on the premise that it would protect consumers against rising rates in the winter, and the consumers would never know the difference. Or, they could inform the consumers that the utility gas rates would not go up in the winter. But then, of course, no one would want to buy their fixed-rate plan.

It didn't take long for them make the call. They felt that it would have been dishonest to offer a fixed-rate plan on what would be a false premise. IEI salespeople would have had to essentially lie through omission in order to actually sell the fixed rates. Darin and Rich pulled their fixed rates off the market that year in New Jersey, which would significantly decrease their growth in the new market. Although the move cost IEI significantly in the short term, it was simply the right thing to do.

Self-Sacrifice: The Ultimate Test of Character

Some companies take this commitment to doing the right thing at all times even further by applying it to how they treat employees. When Aaron Feuerstein took control of fleece-and-textile manufacturer Malden Mills in 1957, he represented the third generation of Feuersteins running this Lawrence, Massachusetts-based company with a reputation for being a great place to work.

Aaron kept the tradition and good name alive by helping other local businesses and offering English classes for local immigrant workers. He also took exceptional care of the employees of his company by ensuring that they had safe, comfortable working conditions and paying them better than most of his competitors.

Apparently, even the unions applauded his efforts and referred to him being "a man of his word" and "extremely compassionate."

But his compassion would be put to an incredible test in December of 1995. At approximately 8:00 on the night of December 11, a boiler exploded at the mill. It was so powerful that it broke gas pipes in the building. The fire, fueled by the gas and the chemicals used in textile manufacturing, spread very quickly. Employees ran out of the buildings. More than 30 of them were injured, several quite badly.

The fire became so powerful that even the efforts of the over 200 firefighters on the scene were essentially futile. The fire raged out of control the entire night, with flames reaching heights of nearly 50 feet. By the time it was out the following morning, Malden Mills had burned to the ground.

The company had a $300 million insurance policy in place for the building. Aaron Feuerstein could have simply ended company operations or closed the Lawrence location and moved to a much less expensive location, as many of the former Lawrence-based mills had done. Almost immediately, though, Aaron announced that he would rebuild the Lawrence location to ensure that the community would not lose one of its largest employers.

But he did more than that. He demonstrated a level of compassion that is almost unheard of in the world of business: He promised to pay employees their full salary while the building was being rebuilt, and he kept his promise. When construction was delayed a couple months later, he announced that the people in his company would still be paid until the project was finished. By the time Malden Mills was up and running again, Aaron had spent roughly $25 million to keep employees on the payroll.

Aaron Feuerstein's compassion would bring him international attention for being a hero. His story was widely reported in the media and he was even acknowledged during one of President Clinton's state of the union addresses. His compassion would also end up costing him control of his company as creditors forced him out and replaced him with a CEO that they felt would move more quickly in terms of getting the company back to being profitable again. Unfortunately, his creditors were only focused on the short-term results.

Despite the apparent short-term disadvantages, companies are much better off in the long run with a leader like Aaron in charge. I'm also confident that Aaron Feuerstein's obituary will be a much better read than that of the CEO with whom his creditors replaced him. Instead of reading something like, "He was really good at hitting the quarterly numbers," Aaron's obituary will read something like, "Aaron Feuerstein was an international hero who inspired hundreds of millions of people with his love and his commitment to being a person of honor and integrity. He always did the right thing, regardless of the personal costs to do so."

10 Measuring the Right Things

In May of 1972, after traveling to the most remote parts of his country with his father, who was the king of Bhutan, the 17-year-old prince named Jigme Singye Wangchuck was put in charge of the country's eastern regions. Only weeks later, on July 21, his father passed away while on a trip to Nairobi, Kenya. The young prince was now king, the youngest monarch in the world, and suddenly responsible for leading the entire nation.

Fortunately for the people of his country, this young king was wise beyond his years. He cared deeply about the people of his nation and their future and, with an uncorrupted beginner's mind, had some very innovative ideas for how to best lead a country. Early in his reign as king, while on a trip through India, a reporter asked King Wangchuck to comment on the size of the gross domestic product (GDP) of Bhutan. His reply would be the spark of a revolution. "Why are we so obsessed with GDP?" he asked. "Why don't we measure gross national happiness?"

This is precisely what he would focus on as the leader of his country. Of course he didn't ignore Bhutan's economy, but his focus was on the overall well-being of the people he led.

To this day, Bhutan continues to measure gross national happiness (GNH), and has developed a plethora of metrics for doing so.[1] For instance, after the questions we're used to seeing on our census questionnaire about basic demographic information, the GNH survey includes questions like:

- What are the six or seven things that you consider to be most important that leads to a happy and contented life?
- How much do you enjoy life?
- What are your main sources of stress?

The revolution that King Jigme Singye Wancghuck sparked was a happy one, and other countries would gradually follow his example. Today, over 40 countries are making efforts to study their GNH.

Measuring the Intangibles in Business

Shortly after September, 11, 2001, while the United States was feeling the effects of the dot-com bust and the terrorist attacks that shocked the nation, Chip Conley asked a question very similar to the one asked by the king of Bhutan so many years earlier. Chip is the founder of a hotel company based in San Francisco called Joie de Vivre,[2] which is French for "joy of life." As such, the vision for Joie de Vivre is to bring more joy to the lives of others through serving their guests.

But Chip was finding it challenging to bring his vision to life. As a result of the struggling economy, Bay area hotels were experiencing the largest decline in revenues in U.S. history. And at the time, many Americans were boycotting all things French because of France's opposition to the invasion of Iraq. We started calling our French fries "freedom fries." This was not a good time to have a name like Joie de Vivre.

On a day when Chip was feeling particularly down about the situation, he went to the bookstore with the intent of looking for some solutions in business books. However, because of his emotional state, he ended up in the self-help section and stumbled upon a book by Abraham Maslow on his famous hierarchy of needs. The book gave him a flash of insight into his customers' and employees' needs. He took the five levels of needs in Maslow's scheme and condensed them to three—survival, success, and transformation—which he calls the *transformation pyramid.*

As his ideas crystallized around the transformation pyramid, Chip realized that Joie de Vivre could do a better job of addressing and meeting the higher needs outlined in the pyramid. It occurred to him that the reason they weren't meeting the higher-level needs of their customers and employees was quite simple: They weren't measuring them. In fact, they had no idea how to measure intangible things like happiness.

Accordingly, Chip set out to create metrics to measure leadership's effectiveness at meeting the higher-level needs of his team. He would later refine these metrics after a visit to Bhutan, where he met with King Jigme Singye Wancghuck and learned about the extensive metrics Bhutan uses to measure GNH. As Chip explains in his great TED talk:

> So we started asking ourselves: What kind of less obvious metrics could we use to actually evaluate our employees' sense of meaning, or our customers' sense of emotional connection with us? For example, we actually started asking our employees: do they understand the mission of our company, and do they feel like they believe in it, can they actually

influence it, and do they feel that their work actually has an impact on it? We started asking our customers [whether or not they felt] an emotional connection with us, in one of seven different kinds of ways. Miraculously, as we asked these questions and started giving attention higher up the pyramid, what we found is that we created more loyalty.... Our customer loyalty skyrocketed. Our employee turnover dropped to one-third of the industry average, and during that five-year dotcom bust we tripled in size."[3]

There's an old and fairly commonsense axiom in business that what gets measured gets done. If management doesn't have metrics for an aspect of the organization, it makes it very hard to develop a plan for improvement. If we don't have a way to measure what success looks like, how can we possibly know how to get there? Also, failing to measure these things sends a message to everyone in the organization that, "This aspect of our organization isn't really that important. If it was, we would measure it and report on the results."

This applies equally in our personal lives. Most of us have goals and ways of measuring our progress when it comes to very practical things, such as daily checklists, annual income, or losing weight. But what we are doing to measure the most important things in our lives, like how strong our relationships are with others, or how well we treat others, or whether we are the person we aspire to be? Are we measuring the right things?

Be Goals versus Do Goals

Most shareholders of publicly traded companies are not measuring the right things. These people tend to care about one thing and one thing only: the market price of their shares. There are many reasons why this is a terrible metric for success. First and foremost, the stock shares' market price has nothing to do with what the company is actually worth. Market prices are based on emotion, not a company's intrinsic value. If there's a market crash, and everyone is scared, even the share price of an incredibly valuable company with great long-term prospects will go down and *stay* down until people's emotional state creates market changes.

This is why Warren Buffett, arguably the greatest investor of all time, often waits years to buy shares of a company that he likes. He is able to determine quite accurately what a company is actually worth. If he determines that Coca-Cola, for instance, is worth $175 billion, but the market has it priced at $180 billion, he is not going to buy. Coca-Cola is overpriced.

Even if he thought the future prospects for Coca-Cola were fantastic, Warren would wait years until he bought Coca-Cola, because he knows that eventually emotions will dictate a cheaper price for the company, which means that he could assure himself of both an immediate profit and the chances for long-term growth. While most "investors" look at share prices daily or even hourly, Buffett is known for checking share prices once a quarter or so. He has often joked how the only time he looks at share prices is when he hears that emotions are strong. That's when he finds good deals, thanks to people who focus on share price as a metric.

Focusing on share price is also problematic for a reason that applies to all organizations, public, private, or even nonprofit: It's a moment-to-moment metric. Focusing on short-term metrics, even quarterly financial reports, can be devastating for an organization's long-term success. Former Medtronic CEO Bill George—who we first introduced in Chapter 9 and who achieved extraordinary business success by every metric—makes it very clear why this is so in his book *Authentic Leadership*.[4]

To put it simply, we eventually fail to serve the customer when we focus on quarterly financials. And no business survives very long without customers. This kind of focus makes us much more likely to want to cut costs than to balance the reduction of expenses with the long-term investments that are absolutely vital for actually serving our customers. As Bill writes, "Inevitably, the short-term opportunities to increase shareholder value taper off. At this point top management usually turns to financial restructuring to achieve its financial goals. Nonstrategic acquisitions, divestitures, consolidations, layoffs, and cutbacks generally follow. By the time these financial moves are completed, the corporation has lost its capacity for growth. Restoring the firm to a growth company at this point is a long, arduous process."

Of course, this is not to say that we shouldn't be aware of our quarterly financial numbers, or that we should eliminate them as a metric. The point is simply that if we want to have consistent long-term growth in our organizations, we can't just focus on short-term financials. We should focus on the underlying elements of the organizations that create the conditions for long-term growth and profitability: happy, loyal employees who ensure that we have happy, loyal customers. And the best way to increase our focus on these things that really matter is to measure them.

We can measure the health of the organization as a whole by asking questions like:

- How happy are you at home?
- How happy are you at work?

- How would you explain the vision and mission of our organization?[5]

- To what degree do you feel your daily work contributes to our vision and mission?

- How well do you feel our organization as a whole lives our core values?

- What can we do to help you enjoy your home life more?

- What can we do to help you enjoy coming to work more?

For the best results, leaders need to ask these questions in face-to-face meetings. An e-mail survey doesn't have nearly the same impact as real human beings asking other human beings questions that show how much we care. Simon Sinek often gives a great example of why this is so important. Imagine that you want to tell your son how much you value him as a member of the family and how much you care about his happiness and success. How well do you think that message would be received if it was delivered via an e-mail? Would he believe you? Our physical presence is essential to show that we actually care about the answers to the questions we're asking.

We can also apply this practice of measuring what really matters to ourselves, and to the organization's other leaders. If we expect our leaders to live our core values and focus on serving those around them, we must measure precisely those things.

As Joel Manby points out in his book *Love Works,* many organizations are great at measuring what he calls *do goals*—the success of the customer experience, employee satisfaction, safety results, brand strength, and financials. But very few measure what Manby calls *be goals*—those we set for how we want our leaders to treat each other and the members of their teams while they are working to accomplish the "do" goals. In essence, the "be" goals measure how well a leader lives the core values and fits in with the culture. Leaders at HFE are not only measured on how well they achieve the "do" goals, but their performance on "be" goals is also important. In fact, their compensation is directly tied to how well they do on both; in order to even qualify to be a senior leader at HFE, a person must excel at both.

To get the best measure of the "be" goals we set for our leaders, we should consider gathering anonymous, 360-degreee feedback from employees and peers, and getting feedback from seniors in person. We can ask questions (reformulated for accurate survey measurement, of course) such as:

- How well does Bob listen?
- How willing is Bob to help others?
- How important to Bob is the happiness and success of the people he leads?
- How kind is Bob?
- How compassionate is Bob?
- How well does Bob live core value A (repeat for each value)?

In essence, we're asking, "How well does Bob love his team?" Of course, we're not talking about some romantic feeling that people often confuse with love. We're talking about *acts* of love—extending oneself for others' benefit and treating them with kindness and compassion. This is what it takes to be the ultimate leader.

When we commit to measuring how well we love those around us, and how well the other leaders in our organization love those around them, we can dramatically improve the business outcomes for our organizations. It's also a very practical way to make the shift toward being the ultimate leader. It helps us focus on the parts of our leadership development that are the most essential for achieving positive long-term business outcomes. And, as I believe we all know deep down inside, how well we love may be the only thing in life that's ultimately worth measuring at all.

Years ago, I read about some fascinating research on near-death experiences (NDEs). An NDE occurs when someone has been pronounced clinically dead by a medical professional for at least a moment or two, or sometimes for 5 or 10 minutes, and then is later revived. In most cases, people who experience an NDE are able to talk about what it was like to be dead.

The research I read included case studies on hundreds of people from around the world who had an NDE. Of course, with such a large sample set, there were many aspects of the experiences that were different for each person. However, what caught my attention was that one aspect of the NDE seemed to be the same in almost every single case in which the person reached the point of possibly permanently leaving the body. As these people died and left their bodies behind on the operating table or other earthly location, they were all asked a question.

Perhaps the most interesting element of all this is that it didn't matter what culture the person came from, how old he was, or what her gender was. In fact, it didn't even matter what the person's religious background was. If he was Christian it was Jesus asking him this question, if he was Muslim it was Allah, if she was agnostic or atheist it was her own deepest self. But in almost every single case, as these people were approaching the boundary between this world and the next, the question was the same: "How well did you love?"

11 Becoming the Ultimate Leader

There was once an emperor who wanted to become the ultimate leader. He thought that if he only knew the answers to three questions, he might become the greatest leader in history. The three questions were:

1. What is the best time to do each thing?
2. Who are the most important people to work with?
3. What is the most important thing to do at all times?

The emperor issued a decree throughout the kingdom announcing that whoever could answer the questions would receive a great reward. Many who read the decree made their way to the palace immediately, with many different answers.

In reply to the first question, one person advised that the emperor make up a thorough time schedule, consecrating every hour, day, month, and year for certain tasks, and then follow that schedule to the letter. Only then could he hope to do every task at the right time.

Another person replied that it was impossible to plan in advance and that the emperor should put all vain amusements aside and remain attentive to all important tasks in order to know what to do at what time.

Someone else insisted that the emperor could never hope to have all the foresight and competence necessary to decide when to do each and every task by himself. This person said that what he really needed was to set up a council of wise men and then act according to their advice.

Someone else said that certain matters required an immediate decision and could not wait for consultation, but if he wanted to know in advance what was going to happen, he could consult magicians and soothsayers.

The responses to the second question also lacked accord. One person told the emperor to place all his trust in administrators, another urged reliance on priests and monks, while others recommended physicians. Still others put their faith in warriors.

The third question drew a similar variety of answers. Some claimed that science was the most important pursuit. Others insisted on religion. Yet others claimed that the most important thing was military skill.

The emperor was not pleased with any of the answers, and gave no reward. After several nights of reflection, the emperor resolved to visit a hermit who lived up on the mountain, who was said to be an enlightened man. The emperor wished to find the hermit and ask him the three questions, though he knew that the hermit never left the mountain and was known to receive only the poor, refusing to have anything to do with persons of wealth or power. So the emperor disguised himself as a simple peasant and ordered his attendants to wait for him at the foot of the mountain while he climbed the slope alone to seek the hermit.

Reaching the holy man's dwelling place, the emperor found the hermit digging a garden in front of his hut. When the hermit saw the stranger, he smiled, nodded his head in greeting, and continued to dig. The labor was obviously hard on him. He was an old man, and each time he thrust his spade into the ground to turn the earth, he grunted heavily.

The emperor approached him and said, "Wise sir, I have come here to ask your help with three questions: When is the best time to do each thing? Who are the most important people to work with? And, what is the most important thing to do at all times?"

The hermit listened attentively but only smiled, patted the emperor on the shoulder and continued digging. The emperor said, "You must be tired. Here, let me give you a hand with that." The hermit thanked him, handed the emperor the spade, and then sat down on the ground to rest.

After he had dug two rows, the emperor stopped and turned to the hermit and repeated his three questions. The hermit still did not answer, but instead stood up and pointed to the spade and said, "Why don't you rest now? I can take over again." But the emperor continued to dig.

One hour passed, then two. Finally the sun began to set behind the mountain. The emperor put down the spade and said to the hermit, "I came here to ask if you could answer my three questions. But if you cannot give me any answer, please tell me so that I can get on my way home."

The hermit lifted his head and asked the emperor, "Do you hear someone running over there?" The emperor turned his head.

They both saw a man with a long, white beard emerge from the woods. He ran wildly, pressing his hands against a bloody wound in his stomach. The man ran toward the emperor before falling unconscious to the ground, where he lay groaning.

Opening the man's clothing, the emperor and the hermit saw that the man had received a deep gash. The emperor cleaned the wound thoroughly and then used his own shirt to bandage it, but the blood completely soaked his shirt within minutes. He rinsed the shirt out and bandaged the wound a second time, and continued this process until the flow of blood had stopped.

The wounded man then regained consciousness and said, "So thirsty." The emperor ran down to the stream, brought back a jug of fresh water, and gave the man a drink. The man fell into a peaceful sleep.

At this point, the sun had disappeared and the night air had begun to turn cold. The hermit and the emperor carried the man into the hut where they laid him down on the hermit's bed. The emperor was exhausted from a long day climbing the mountain, digging the garden, and helping the wounded man. Leaning against the doorway, he fell asleep.

When the emperor awoke, the sun had already risen over the mountain. For a moment he forgot where he was and what he had come for. He looked over to the bed and saw the wounded man also looking around him in confusion. When the man saw the emperor, he stared at him intently and then said in a faint whisper, "Please forgive me."

"But what have you done that I should forgive you?" the emperor asked.

"You do not know me, your majesty, but I know you. I was your sworn enemy and I had vowed to take vengeance on you, for during the last war you killed my brother and seized my property. When I learned that you were coming here alone to the mountain to meet the hermit, I resolved to surprise you on your way back and kill you. But after waiting a long time there was still no sign of you, so I left my place of ambush in order to seek you out."

"But instead of finding you I came across your attendants, who recognized me, giving me this wound. Luckily I escaped and ran here. If I hadn't met you I would surely be dead by now. I had intended to kill you, but instead you saved my life! I am deeply ashamed and also grateful beyond words. If I live, I vow to be your servant for the rest of my life, and I will bid my children and grandchildren to do the same. Please grant me your forgiveness."

The emperor was overjoyed to see that he was so easily reconciled with a former enemy. He not only forgave the man but promised to return all the man's property and to send his own physician and servants to wait on the man until he was completely healed. After ordering his attendants to take the man home, the emperor returned to see the hermit. Before returning to the palace, the emperor wanted to repeat his three questions one last time. He found the hermit sowing seeds in the earth they had dug the day before.

The hermit knew what he was going to ask, and with a warm smile said, "But your questions have already been answered."

"How's that?" the emperor asked, puzzled.

"Yesterday, if you had not taken pity on my age and given me a hand with digging these beds, you would have been attacked by

that man on your way home. Then you would have deeply regret-
ted not staying with me. Therefore, the most important time was
the time you were digging in the beds, the most important person
was myself, and the most important pursuit was to help me."

"Later, when the wounded man ran up here, the most important time was the time you spent dressing his wound, for if you
had not cared for him he would have died. At a minimum, you
would have never known the joy of reconciliation with a former
enemy. And, it's quite possible that the man would have tried to
attack you again in the future. Thus, he was the most important
person, and the most important pursuit was taking care of his
wound."

"Remember that there is only one important time, and that
is *now*. The present moment is the only time over which we have
dominion. The most important person is always the person you
are with, who is right before you, for who knows if you will ever
have dealings with any other person in the future? The most
important pursuit is making the person standing at your side
happy, for that alone is the sole pursuit of life."[1]

Becoming the Ultimate Leader Is Enjoyable

This story serves as a great reminder of what we need to do to be
most effective as leaders, and in our lives in general. Simply being
fully present with a person is one of the most effective ways to
show that we care. In fact, being fully present with *what* we're
doing now and *who* we're with in this moment may just be the
most important thing we can do in our lives.

Fortunately, being fully present in each moment is something we can train to do—and that training is not at all arduous.

It's actually very enjoyable. Mindfulness training, which I discussed briefly in Part One, is the practice of being fully present now while also developing the wisdom that allows us to be fully present more easily in the future. In any moment of our training that we actually achieve the perspective of mindfulness—which is simply being aware, without judgment, of our thoughts, emotional state, and what's coming in through our physical senses—we discover a little miracle: We are happy.

In addition to the anecdotal evidence—for example, my story of realizing true happiness with nothing while confined to the brig—there is also a large body of research demonstrating just how effective mindfulness training is for increasing our baseline levels of happiness; that is, happiness that doesn't depend on what happens to us. Some of the research includes studies in which people self-report on their levels of happiness. But there is also brain scan research, using fMRI technology, to measure very objectively how happy subjects are. In one study, researchers looked at a long-time practitioner of mindfulness versus a large control group to determine the ability to generate brain activity in the area of the brain most associated with happiness. The mindfulness practitioner was Matthieu Ricard. As mentioned in Chapter 6, the researchers stated that they had found the happiest person, by far, ever measured by science.

It is clearly good news that practicing mindfulness as a key element of training to become the ultimate leader is inherently enjoyable, since this makes us more likely to stick with it. It's also very good for the people around us. If we are happy, we are much more likely to see and act on opportunities to help others. As Shawn Achor points out in his excellent book *The Happiness Advantage*, leaders in more positive moods are also better able to think creatively, problem solve, negotiate, and even influence higher performance from employees.[2]

Staying Cool under Pressure

Who would you rather follow: a leader who gets easily frazzled by even mildly stressful situations, or a leader who stays cool even in very challenging situations? The question is clearly rhetorical. The ability to stay calm and collected under pressure makes us much more effective and it inspires confidence in the people around us. In fact, there is a large body of evidence suggesting that one's ability to successfully manage emotions is the single most important ingredient for high levels of performance, especially as a leader.

Years ago, Daniel Goleman, the bestselling author of *Emotional Intelligence*,[3] conducted a now-famous study involving people from 188 large, global companies. He wanted to uncover the most important ingredient of successful leadership defined in several ways, including profit, employee turnover, and so forth. He found something pretty remarkable: Regardless of how one defined successful leadership, the research showed that emotional intelligence was far and away the most important ingredient for success. In fact, it was twice as important as IQ or technical skills for achieving success as a leader.

Another benefit of mindfulness practice is that it is perhaps the most important tool there is for developing emotional intelligence. One of the most popular in-house training programs at Google is a mindfulness-based emotional intelligence program called "Search inside Yourself." The program has been so successful that the co-creator, Chade-Meng Tan (Meng), decided to write a book by the same name.[4] The book became a *New York Times* best-seller, and Meng founded the Search Inside Yourself

Leadership Institute (SIYLI, pronounced *silly*),[5] which now offers the program to organizations outside of Google.

There are now numerous other companies that train employees in mindfulness, including Apple, Deutsche Bank, Procter & Gamble, Astra Zeneca, Facebook, Twitter, Intel, Raytheon, General Mills, and Aetna, just to name a few. Even the U.S. military is now offering mindfulness training. The military has seen the evidence, and is highly interested in helping their service members increase stress resilience. They know how critical it is to develop leaders who can stay cool, think clearly, and act decisively under the most extreme of circumstances.

The Ultimate Tool for Becoming the Ultimate Leader

Over the past 40 years, a tremendous body of research has accumulated demonstrating many benefits, in addition to those previously mentioned, of regular mindfulness training. There are so many benefits to the practice that it would be rather easy to draw the conclusion that mindfulness training is the single most important thing we can do for our personal development. Following is just a partial list of documented benefits of the practice:

- More fluid adaptation to change and development of more effective coping strategies
- Improved concentration
- Improved creativity
- Improved social skills
- Increased working memory
- Improved planning and organizational skills
- Increased self-esteem

- Increased sense of calmness, relaxation, and self-acceptance
- More accepting attitude toward life and its challenges
- Improved immune system functioning
- Lasting decreases in a variety of stress-related physical symptoms, including chronic pain
- Significant decreases in anxiety and depression
- Increased quality of sleep

As beneficial as the practice is in so many ways, what makes mindfulness training such a vital tool for becoming the ultimate leader is the wisdom that develops a result of the practice.

Regular mindfulness practice makes our abilities to orient and sustain awareness increasingly strong. Our awareness becomes like a bright spotlight that sees whatever passes through it, including our thoughts and emotions, with incredible clarity. And this increased clarity allows us to regularly see something that very few people see: the cessation of a thought.

Intellectually, we all know that thoughts don't remain permanently in our conscious minds. They come up, hang around for a bit, and then pass away. But very few people ever see the cessation of a thought with their own awareness. For most of us, the mind seems to be a constant flow of images and our own inner voice chattering away. We live as though we *are* our thinking—especially the voice inside the mind.

But just a little bit of mindfulness training allows us to see a thought arising in the mind very clearly. We watch it becoming fully conscious, and then fading away, leaving a mind that is completely clear of thought. This results in an incredible insight: We recognize that our thoughts, including those coming from that voice in our heads, are conditioned phenomena that simply arise and pass away in the mind. We see that we are there before a thought arises, while it is present in the mind, and after it is gone. More than just understanding intellectually, we *know* that we are not our thinking.

With regular practice—for which there's a brief guide in the Appendix—we can have this insight frequently. And each time we do, we become a little less attached to the thoughts that arise and pass away in the mind. We see them more as tools that help us navigate through our world instead of seeing them as what we are. This allows us to gradually become free from the ego. The ego, which comprises nothing but thought, is that part of ourselves that always puts our needs above others' needs. The more attached we are to it, the more self-centered we are. And, of course, the more self-centered we are, the less effective we will be as leaders.

The ultimate leader is essentially selfless. Because she is no longer attached to her ego, she sees both her own needs and the needs of those around her not as two separate things, but as one and the same. This allows her to always think in terms of what is best for the greater good, not just for herself. She no longer has to make an effort to devote herself to caring for and serving the people around her. It becomes her natural response.

Part of the large body of research demonstrating how effective mindfulness training is for becoming free from the ego includes another fascinating study using fMRI brain scans.[6] In the study, researchers measured a long-time mindfulness practitioner's ability to generate brain activity in the left prefrontal cortex—the area of the brain most associated with compassion—against a control group of 150 people. The results were unbelievable.

The long-time mindfulness practitioner ended up two standard deviations outside of the bell curve. This is an outlier to an outlier, literally off the chart (and then off of whatever other chart he landed on). Any reasonable researcher would assume that a measurement error had occurred and redo this experiment. But studies like this have been replicated numerous times with similar results.

In fact, it was later learned that mindfulness practitioners have higher baseline levels of activity in the left prefrontal cortex. It turns out that mindfulness training actually makes physical changes to the brain's structure, resulting in an increased ability to be more kind and compassionate. Fortunately for us, we don't need to practice for thousands of hours to see improvement. We can see positive changes in the brain after as little as eight weeks of training.

It is clear that practicing mindfulness as often as we can makes it easier to live a life devoted to serving others. Also, each moment of practice is actually an act of service to others. In any moment that we actually achieve the perspective of mindfulness, we are happy and at peace, which in and of itself is a service to those around us. We also become a little less attached to the ego, which means that we move a little closer to becoming people whose natural responses to those around them are kindness, compassion, generosity, and service—we move a little closer to becoming the ultimate leader.

Making a Profit While Making a Difference

Applying mindfulness, and the other tools we've discussed for becoming the ultimate leader, can certainly help us to achieve the extraordinary business outcomes like those mentioned throughout this book. But becoming a leader who is devoted to more effectively serving and caring for others can do even more than that. When we look closely, we can see that by working to become the ultimate leaders, we can have a significant positive impact on the entire world.

If you and your organization achieve high levels of success by focusing on serving the people on your team and your community, other people and organizations will want to copy you. If enough organizations demonstrate that you can be much more successful over the long term by focusing on serving others, it would become the norm. Learning how to more effectively serve others would be required coursework in any business school worth attending. Gradually, it would become common knowledge that if we focus on seeking out entertainment and accumulating money and possessions, our chances are slim for leading a truly enjoyable, meaningful, and successful life. Leading such a life is the result of focusing on serving others and the greater good.

Can you imagine how such a cultural shift would affect our world? If serving others and serving the greater good become the standard model for high levels of long-term success, things like poverty and violence would gradually disappear.

For those of us who doubt that just one person like us could actually make a substantial impact on the world, let's consider the power of cause and effect as outlined by the so-called butterfly effect. Most of us have likely heard of this analogy that scientists use to help us understand how small, local events result in large, global events. An example of the butterfly effect begins with a butterfly flapping her wings in the Amazonian jungle. This results in a fly changing its course, which results in a bird eating the fly and returning to his nest a little bit earlier. After a long chain of events, we see that the end result is a change in the global weather pattern known as El Niño.

While this may be an analogy, it is certainly not fantasy. These types of scenarios are observed every day in laboratories of all types and they are playing themselves out continuously in each moment of existence.

So this is my question to you: If a butterfly flapping her wings can result in a change in the global weather pattern, what could happen with just one act of extending yourself for the benefit of those around you?

There's no doubt that it will help you and your organization to be more successful. And, even more important, you might just change the world.

AFTERWORD

I truly believe that you can achieve extraordinary success as a leader while simultaneously making a significant, positive impact on the world. However, this is possible only if you take action. So before you put this book down and move on to what's next, please take a moment to write down at least three things you will do in the next 24 hours to help you better serve the people around you and inspire others to do the same.

One very easy first step is to commit to start at least a little bit of mindfulness training. You can find instructions for doing that in the Appendix.

Even easier, if you found this book helpful and inspiring, you could make a list of the people you think would benefit from reading it, and share it with them.

Together, we can build a worldwide community of highly effective leaders who are devoted to serving and inspiring greatness in others—we can change the world.

AUTHOR'S NOTE

All of the author proceeds from the sale of this book will be donated to the charities supported through a program implemented by my company, called Project Share.

Part of my transition from being mostly selfish to being as selfless as I can be has included making an effort to keep only what I need to be healthy, and to share anything extra. I apply this both in my personal life and in my company.

Accordingly, each time I am hired by a client, we offer to donate 10 percent of the speaking fee to that client's favorite charity. We see this as an opportunity to offer a gentle reminder of both the power and the joy of being generous.

Also, we are committed to keeping only what we need for the business and ourselves, and sharing the rest. At the end of each tax year, we donate 100 percent of profits that are not needed to keep the business viable. Necessary expenses include paying employees fair but not excessive salaries (I limit my salary to what I need to support the basic needs of my household), basic business expenses, and retaining enough capital to cover three to six months of those operational expenses. Everything else is donated to my favorite nonprofit organizations. You can see which organizations we support at www.MattTenney.com.

Our current goal is to donate at least $50,000 by the end of 2014 to nonprofit organizations doing great work.

I envision a world where every company operates with a similar model: instead of using profit as a means to accumulate wealth and possessions, using it to serve the people in the organization and the community. This not only results in better business outcomes, but it simply makes life more awesome.

I hope that you'll consider sharing with those around you in the same way. If you're already doing so, I'd love to hear about your experiences.

In service,
Matt Tenney

SERVE YOUR TEAM

If you are interested in serving the members of your team by offering them leadership, ethics, or sales keynotes or training programs based on the principles in *Serve to Be Great*, please visit:

www.MattTenney.com

If you are interested in placing a bulk order of *Serve to Be Great* at a discount for large groups or for your organization, please contact your favorite bookseller or Wiley Special Sales at:

SpecialSales@wiley.com or 800-762-2974

CONNECT WITH MATT

To sign up for Matt Tenney's eZine, please visit: www.MattTenney.com

If you have questions or comments for Matt, you can reach him via the following social media:

Twitter: @MattTenney1

LinkedIn: /Matt-Tenney

Facebook: /MattTenneyServes

ABOUT THE AUTHOR

Matt Tenney is an international keynote speaker, a trainer, and a consultant with the prestigious Perth Leadership Institute, whose clients include numerous Fortune 500 companies. He works with companies, associations, universities, and nonprofits to develop highly effective leaders who achieve lasting success by focusing on serving and inspiring greatness in the people around them. Matt envisions a world in which the vast majority of people realize that effectively serving others is the key to true greatness. When he's not traveling for speaking engagements, he can often be found in Nashville, Tennessee.

ACKNOWLEDGMENTS

There are countless people I would like to thank for their help throughout my life, without whom I surely would not be doing the work I do. For the sake of brevity here, I would like to acknowledge and thank those who have had the greatest impact on the success of this book.

First, I'd like to thank *you*, the reader. Without people like you, who seek to become better leaders and better human beings, this book would not exist. Thank you for helping to make our world a better place by making the statement, through the act of reading this book and applying the ideas within it, that true greatness in leadership and in life is achieved by focusing on serving others.

Thank you to my parents. Without their unconditional support, this book never would have come to be.

Thank you to my wonderful fiancée and best friend, Leah. She inspires me every day with her incredible thoughtfulness, her care for the people around her, and her devotion to being as Christlike as possible.

Thank you to Jon Gordon, who is one of the most selfless people I have ever met. Despite an incredibly busy schedule, he took the time to introduce me to the publishing team at John Wiley & Sons, and he did not hesitate when I asked him to write the Foreword for this book.

Thank you to Simon Sinek for believing in me, and for taking time out of his incredibly busy schedule to mentor me and to introduce me to so many great people, including Charlie Kim, whose company was a significant source of inspiration and evidence for the ideas shared in this book.

Thank you to the other mentors in my life who played a significant role in helping this book come to be: Michael Carroll, John Spence, Ted Prince, and Peter Chatel.

Thank you to Matt Holt and Shannon Vargo at John Wiley & Sons for taking a chance on me, and believing that this book would help leaders to become more effective and to make more of a positive impact on our world. Thanks to Shannon for being so gentle with my naïveté and so patient with my endless questions. Thanks to both Shannon and Christine Moore for all the time spent working to make this book so much better than it was in its infancy. Thanks to Liz Gildea for jumping right in on this project so soon after starting with Wiley and working to help everything come together. Thanks to Linda Indig for being so patient and flexible in the face of my naïveté and some very tight deadlines. Thanks to Peter Knox for all the great marketing support (and for introducing me to John Sampieri, the jeweler who made the engagement ring of Leah's dreams). Thanks to the design team who made the eye-catching cover for this book.

Thank you to Susan Liimatta, who requested that I create a program specifically on the topic of servant leadership for the National Center for Student Leadership Conference she plans. As a result of her request, I made a subtle shift in how I present the ideas I share. This simple shift in focus has been instrumental in reaching more people with my speaking, and led to the writing of this book.

Thank you to Arianna Huffington for inviting me to write for the *Huffington Post*, which gave me a big platform early in my career to share the message that serving others is the key to true greatness.

Thank you to Cyndi Maxey for showing me how to write a great book proposal.

Thank you to all those who took the time out of their very busy schedules to write endorsements for this book because they believe in the message: John Spence, Ted Prince, Michael Carroll, Chade-Meng Tan, Adam Grant, Mark Sanborn, Chip Conley, Mark C. Crowley, Dan Black, Chris Marcell Murchison, Simon Sinek, Skip Prichard, Jon Gordon, Clifton L. Taulbert, Jeff Klein, and David Marquet.

APPENDIX:
A QUICK START GUIDE TO
MINDFULNESS TRAINING

To summarize mindfulness training very briefly, there are essentially two aspects:

1. We train our awareness so that we become less distracted by our own thinking, which allows us to enjoy our lives more, to be more present with people, and to see our world, both inner and outer, with greater clarity.

2. We apply that clearer awareness to investigate reality and develop the wisdom that frees us from attachment to the ego, which increases both our happiness and our ability to serve others more effectively.

Awareness Training in Activity

The easiest way to begin is to transform activities that we already do each day into opportunities to be happier while simultaneously training ourselves to become more effective at serving others. Let's use drinking water or coffee at work as an example. Before beginning the act of drinking, we simply note mentally the word *drinking,* and then give our full attention to the act of drinking, exploring what the experience is like.

We make the effort to let go of trying to think about things, and simply explore the experience of drinking—the sensation of the cup in our hands; the sight of what's in view; the sensations of the liquid first touching the lips, entering the mouth, and going down the throat; and the sound of swallowing. It's perfectly okay if thoughts come up. We just recognize them, allow them to come and go, and keep our awareness alive to what's coming in through our senses.

I recommend making a list of all the things you have to do each day both at work and at home—things that don't require you to think actively, like drinking, washing your hands, brushing your teeth, walking to the bathroom on breaks, eating, walking to your car, and so on. Then pick one activity and make a commitment to be mindful and aware during that activity each time you engage in it for one week.

At the end of the week, it should be almost second nature to be mindful during the activity you chose. For week two, continue with the first activity and commit to a second one. Each week, you continue with the activities you are already practicing with and add another.

After a few months, you may find that you are practicing awareness training during all of the times that don't require you to intentionally analyze, plan, or otherwise think (you might be surprised at how much of your life doesn't require thinking, and how much of it you've been missing because you're caught up in your thinking). During the times that don't require thinking, you might find that your default has switched from almost constantly thinking (the default for most of us) to being much more aware of what's coming in through your senses, which is a simple side effect of not intentionally thinking and not being distracted by the thoughts that automatically arise in the mind.

Awareness Training in Stillness

We can also train our awareness while sitting still. This is a very important aspect of the training, because wisdom is much more likely to develop while we are still than when we are in motion.

To practice awareness training while sitting still, apply the same effort you do during activity. Simply explore what it is like to be alive and breathing while sitting still. Although you may choose to have a training session while sitting still for one minute, or five minutes, or 25 minutes, don't worry about maintaining awareness without distraction for the entire training session. The only goal is to be aware of what is coming in through your senses for the duration of one in-breath, and then again for one out-breath. It's just one breath at a time.

With each breath, simply keep the attitude of *What's happening now?* There may be a lot of thinking, or the mind may be clear. You may be happy, or you may be angry. It doesn't matter what is happening. Your only goal is to explore, nonjudgmentally, what is coming in through your senses. If you find yourself distracted by thinking, you can simply recognize that and allow yourself to reestablish your attitude of *What's happening now?* with the next breath.

I recommend committing to at least one minute of sitting still practice each morning and evening. You will likely find the practice relaxing and want to add more. You can gradually add more time based on what's realistic for you. The ideal time for a session is at least 10 minutes each morning and evening.

When you train while sitting still for about 10 minutes, you'll find that you gradually start to see your thoughts and emotions more clearly. You may find that you can welcome a thought, look right at it, and see it fade away. This will allow you to see very clearly the impermanence of your thoughts and emotions. This gives rise to the wisdom that you are not your thoughts and emotions—they are simply impermanent conditions that arise and pass away.

Intellectually, we all know this is true. But just knowing something intellectually does not affect how we actually behave. Only direct experience, or wisdom, can change how we operate in the world.

This is why it is so important to practice awareness training consistently and take time to train while sitting still. With training, we become less distracted and our awareness becomes more focused. Gradually, instead of being like a dull light, awareness becomes like a laser beam that cuts away at our attachment to our own thinking. The freer we are from attachment to our thinking, the happier we are, the more effective our minds are, and the more we let go of our self-centered tendencies. All of this serves to help us be much more effective at serving others.

NOTES

Introduction

1. www.fastcompany.com/34512/war-talent.

Chapter 2 From Selfish to Servant

1. www.reicherthouse.org.

2. http://kidskickingcancer.org/.

3. www.artsinmedicine.ufhealth.org.

4. www.kkcgainesville.org.

5. www.Southwest.com.

6. www.hfecorp.com.

7. http://joelmanby.com/.

8. www.jameshunter.com/.

9. www.perthleadership.org.

Chapter 3 Winning the War for Talent

1. www.charitywater.org.

2. https://www.nextjump.com/.

3. I discovered that Next Jump is an e-commerce company. They create customized websites for organizations that allow them to offer incentives for their employees, including special

pricing on merchandise from numerous retailers. I also learned that they aspire to become the largest provider of corporate intranets and that most Fortune 1000 companies are already clients of Next Jump.

4. www.youtube.com/watch?v=498jIXVw4Tg&feature =youtu.be.

5. www.salary.com/wasted-time-at-work-still-costing-companies-billions-in-2006/.

Chapter 4 Creating a Highly Innovative Culture

1. http://www.perthleadership.org/index.php/perth-publication/publications/book-the-three-financial-styles-of-very-successful -leaders.

2. You can see the video at: www.youtube.com/watch?v =vJG698U2Mvo.

3. Stuart Sutherland, *Irrationality: The Enemy Within*, 2nd ed. (London: Pinter & Martin, 2007); Dan Ariely, *Predictably Irrational: The Hidden Forces That Shape Our Decisions* (New York: HarperCollins, 2008), 304. See also http://en.wikipedia.org/wiki/Cognitive_bias.

4. www.cisco.com/.

5. www.google.com/about/company/.

6. www.sas.com.

7. Jeffrey Cohn, Jon Katzenbach, and Gus Vlak, "Finding and Grooming Breakthrough Innovators," *Harvard Business Review* (December 2008).

8. www.fastcompany.com/3004953/how-sas-became-worlds -best-place-work.

Chapter 5 Delivering World-Class Customer Service

1. www.huffingtonpost.com/2012/12/21/zappos-10-hour-call
   _n_2345467.html.

2. http://newsroom.accenture.com/article_display.cfm?article
   _id=4769.

3. http://about.americanexpress.com/news/pr/2010/barometer
   .aspx.

4. Steve Downton, Hilbrand Rustema, and Jan van Veen, "Service Economics: Profitable Growth with a Brand-Driven Service Strategy," Noventum Service Management Consultants Ltd., August 1, 2010, 15–16.

5. www.dbmarketing.com/articles/Art183.htm.

6. www.cbsnews.com/news/top-10-companies-for-customer
   -service/.

7. http://hbswk.hbs.edu/archive/801.html.

8. J. W. Wiley and S. Brooks, "The High Performance Organizational Climate," in Handbook of Organizational Culture and Climate, ed. N. Ashkanasy, C. Wilderom, and M. Peterson (Thousand Oaks, CA: Sage, 2000).

9. www.dailymail.co.uk/news/article-1346716/Airline-pilot
   -holds-plane-family-murdered-toddler.html#ixzz2WCZ
   z1NBb.

10. http://news.travel.aol.com/2011/01/13/pilot-holds-plane
    -for-grandfather-of-murdered-toddler/.

Chapter 6 Why Serving Others Is a Highly Effective Marketing Tactic

1. http://blog.nextjump.com/culture/a-new-philanthropy
   -donating-our-best-asset-our.html.

2. www.Lifeisgood.com.

3. You can watch the video at www.youtube.com/watch?v =lcqCAqZtedI.

4. You can watch the video at www.youtube.com/watch?v=nC _vXAF-pBM.

5. www.ibtimes.com/worlds-happiest-man-matthieu-ricard -credits-meditation-learning-memory-abilities-855856.

Chapter 7 Making Serving a Habit

1. www.awesomelysimple.com/about-the-book.

2. http://jeffreykrames.com/books-by-jk/what-the-best-ceos -know/.

Chapter 8 Grow by Empowering Others

1. www.huffingtonpost.com/chris-hurn/stuffed-giraffe-shows -wha_b_1524038.html.

2. www.fourhourworkweek.com/.

3. www.danpink.com/books/drive.

4. https://www.stephencovey.com/7habits/7habits.php.

5. Joel Manby, *Love Works* (Grand Rapids, MI: Zondervan, 2012).

6. http://holacracy.org/.

7. http://maestroconference.com/.

Chapter 9 Inspire Greatness

1. Simon Sinek, *Start with Why* (New York: Portfolio, 2009), www.startwithwhy.com/.

2. www.ted.com/talks/simon_sinek_how_great_leaders_inspire _action.html.

3. www.medtronic.com/.

4. www.billgeorge.org/page/authentic-leadership1.

5. http://studentmaid.com/.

6. www.jameshunter.com/books.htm.

7. www.infiniteenergy.com/.

Chapter 10 Measuring the Right Things

1. You can see the entire survey at: www.grossnationalhappiness .com.

2. www.jdvhotels.com/.

3. www.ted.com/talks/chip_conley_measuring_what_makes _life_worthwhile.html.

4. www.billgeorge.org/page/authentic-leadership1.

5. Mission refers to what we do to serve our customers. Vision refers to how the world will be positively changed as a result of our products or services. For example, at the speaking and training company I founded, Wanna Save the World, Inc, our mission is to provide both the inspiration and evidence-based tools to help people become highly effective leaders who serve and inspire greatness in others. Our vision is of a world in which the vast majority of people and organizations realize that focusing on serving others is the most effective way to achieve lasting success, which we believe would create the conditions for a permanent end to poverty and violence.

Chapter 11 Becoming the Ultimate Leader

1. Variation of a story originally told by Leo Tolstoy entitled "The Three Questions."

2. Shawn Achor, *The Happiness Advantage* (New York: Crown Publishing Group, 2010), 15, 208, http://goodthinkinc.com/the-happiness-advantage/.

3. www.danielgoleman.info/topics/emotional-intelligence/.

4. www.siybook.com/.

5. www.siyli.org/.

6. www.ted.com/talks/matthieu_ricard_on_the_habits_of _happiness.html.

INDEX